# MOTHER TERESA

# MOTHER TERESA

## A Biography

Meg Greene

GREENWOOD BIOGRAPHIES

**GREENWOOD PRESS**
WESTPORT, CONNECTICUT · LONDON

**Library of Congress Cataloging-in-Publication Data**

Greene, Meg.
    Mother Teresa :  a biography / Meg Greene Malvasi.
        p. cm.—(Greenwood biographies, ISSN 1540–4900)
    Includes index.
    ISBN 0–313–32771–8 (alk. paper)
    1. Teresa, Mother, 1910–  2. Missionaries of Charity—Biography. 3. Nuns—India—
Calcutta—Biography. I. Title. II. Series.
BX4406.5.Z8G74    2004
271'.97—dc22          2004009232

British Library Cataloguing in Publication Data is available.

Library of Congress Catalog Card Number: 2004009232
ISBN: 0–313–32771–8
ISSN: 1540–4900

First published in 2004

Greenwood Press, 88 Post Road West, Westport, CT 06881
An imprint of Greenwood Publishing Group, Inc.
www.greenwood.com

Printed in the United States of America

∞™

The paper used in this book complies with the
Permanent Paper Standard issued by the National
Information Standards Organization (Z39.48–1984).

10  9  8  7  6  5  4  3  2  1

# CONTENTS

Photo essay follows page 66.

# SERIES FOREWORD

In response to high school and public library needs, Greenwood developed this distinguished series of full-length biographies specifically for student use. Prepared by field experts and professionals, these engaging biographies are tailored for high school students who need challenging yet accessible biographies. Ideal for secondary school assignments, the length, format and subject areas are designed to meet educators' requirements and students' interests.

Greenwood offers an extensive selection of biographies spanning all curriculum related subject areas including social studies, the sciences, literature and the arts, history and politics, as well as popular culture, covering public figures and famous personalities from all time periods and backgrounds, both historic and contemporary, who have made an impact on American and/or world culture. Greenwood biographies were chosen based on comprehensive feedback from librarians and educators. Consideration was given to both curriculum relevance and inherent interest. The result is an intriguing mix of the well known and the unexpected, the saints and the sinners from long-ago history and contemporary pop culture. Readers will find a wide array of subject choices from fascinating crime figures like Al Capone to inspiring pioneers like Margaret Mead, from the greatest minds of our time like Stephen Hawking to the most amazing success stories of our day like J. K. Rowling.

While the emphasis is on fact, not glorification, the books are meant to be fun to read. Each volume provides in-depth information about the subject's life from birth through childhood, the teen years, and adulthood. A thorough account relates family background and education, traces personal and professional influences, and explores struggles, accomplishments, and contributions. A timeline highlights the most significant life events against a historical perspective. Bibliographies supplement the reference value of each volume.

# PREFACE

Writing about Mother Teresa can be both a frustrating and challenging exercise. On the surface, she appears almost one-dimensional, living a simple life devoted to her calling and her faith. Closer inspection, however, reveals a personality so rife with contradictions that it is difficult to explain her motives and purposes. What is the reality? What finally can a biographer conclude about the life of Mother Teresa?

In many ways, Mother Teresa defies the biographer's art. Her life is not interesting. There are, or seem to be, no great adventures, no great crises, no great sorrows, no great turning points. Most biographies of her are so reverential and so one-dimensional, that it is easy to forget that she was a human being and did not from birth belong to the ages. Even a list of her numerous accomplishments and awards does little to capture her inner life. She did not appear to suffer from the terrible internal conflicts, hardships, or adversities that often mark a great and memorable life. Rather, her life was mundane and ordinary, and she never pretended it to be otherwise. Perhaps, though, her very ordinariness provides a starting point for the biographer. How did this unexceptional woman captivate and console so many that she has come to take her place among the monumental personalities of the age?

Mother Teresa, however, was something of an artful dodger. When asked about most any topic, but especially herself, she uttered platitudes and pieties that sounded almost meaningless. She concealed herself behind them. Yet, coming from her, these expressions had a ring of truth. That may be because the story of Mother Teresa is not the story of a great life in the modern sense. Mother Teresa was not a celebrity. On the contrary, hers was a life lived on a different principle. She devoted herself to an old-fashioned sense of calling. She worked among the poor of Calcutta because she believed it is what God required of her. She would have done the same work in anonymity if she herself had lived and died in obscurity. It is that devotion that makes the life of Mother Teresa so interesting.

# INTRODUCTION

Modern popular culture promotes celebrity: people who are well known for being well known. Stirring up controversy or scandal and then talking or writing about it enhances celebrity status. Yet, the cult of celebrity does not and cannot adequately explain the hold that a tiny nun from Albania had, and retains, on the conscience of the world.

For a woman who neither sought nor expected recognition, Mother Teresa has exercised an enormous influence around the world. Her missionary work on behalf of the poorest of the poor in India was larger than life, giving rise to questions about how her own experiences prepared her to carry it out and to accomplish all that she did. By all accounts, Mother Teresa was intelligent but passive and self-effacing. She had been an adequate but undistinguished teacher, a commonplace woman, and an ordinary nun, prone to knocking over candles during religious services. Yet, Mother Teresa had one attribute that set her apart in a world often forgetful of God: a deep, abiding faith.

Yet, even Mother Teresa, it seems, could not escape the cult of celebrity, though she tried always to use it to the advantage of the poor whom she served. Until the last decade of her life, Mother Teresa enjoyed universal acclaim as a living saint. Although she appeared indifferent to the attention, she was aware of it and, for example, allowed the media to publish poignant photographs of her working among the poor and the dying to illustrate their plight. Her interview with British journalist Malcolm Muggeridge in 1968 exposed her world to the rest of the world. The public reaction to her work was more than she ever imagined. Donations poured in. But for all the publicity the interview with Muggeridge garnered for her mission, it may also have set her on the slippery slope that is the price of success: Mother Teresa was becoming famous and all that she did, every word that she uttered, was now for public consumption. For good or ill, she was no longer a devout nun laboring in obscurity.

In its appetite for a saintly celebrity, the media scrutinized every aspect of Mother Teresa's life and work. When charges of wrongdoing surfaced, public opinion, the fickle engine that drives the cult of celebrity, turned against Mother Teresa. Some were dismayed; others were angry and disappointed. Cynics everywhere rejoiced that another icon had been smashed. Common faults and foibles were magnified in the public persona of Mother Teresa that the media now brought before the court of public opinion. How could a saint also be stubborn, controlling, and unrealistic? Perhaps Mother Teresa had made a devil's bargain. She had allowed herself to become well known to publicize her cause, while personally shunning the worldly trappings that accompany celebrity. Suddenly, she seemed not only cranky and demanding, but also hypocritical. At the same time, her unswerving belief in the doctrines of the Catholic Church and her traditional view of the subordinate role of women within it made her a target of liberal doctrinaires. Nevertheless, with all the twists and turns that celebrity brings, Mother Teresa was unswerving in her belief that she was an instrument of God.

So, for all her apparent simplicity, and with all that has been said and written about her, it is still easy to misunderstand Mother Teresa. People in the United States and Europe mistook her for a social reformer, determined to rid the world of poverty and injustice. They were disappointed to find out that she was not intent to bring about social change. She doubtless wanted to help and comfort the poor. More important, Mother Teresa sought to bear witness, to show that even on the wretched streets of Calcutta under the worst imaginable conditions, one could encounter God's grace and love.

In 2003, Pope John Paul II beatified Mother Teresa, the final stage on her journey to sainthood. For many who admired her, canonization was a mere formality; Mother Teresa was already a saint. But her beatification has not silenced critics. Many have, in fact, become more strident, hoping to delay or halt her canonization. There is thus considerable justification for additional study of her life and her work. This biography, then, is not only an examination of Mother Teresa's life, but of the beliefs that shaped it. The two are so closely intertwined that not to examine them together is to risk missing some essential aspect of this ordinary extraordinary woman.

# TIMELINE: SIGNIFICANT EVENTS IN MOTHER TERESA'S LIFE

| | |
|---|---|
| 1900 | Nikola Bojaxhiu (father) and his bride, Drana (mother), move to Skopje in Macedonia; Nikola starts a prosperous construction business and moves his wife to a home near the Vardar River. |
| 1905 | Aga Bojaxhiu, sister, is born. |
| 1908 | Lazar Bojaxhiu, brother, is born. |
| 26 August 1910 | Agnes Gonxha Bojaxhiu (Mother Teresa) is born. |
| 1913 | The Balkan Wars end; Macedonia is divided between Serbia, Greece, and Bulgaria. |
| 1919 | Nikola Bojaxhiu dies of suspicious causes. |
| 1925 | Gonxha first becomes interested in mission work, particularly in India. |
| 29 November 1928 | Leaves home to join the Loreto Sisters; she travels to the convent at Rathfarnham near Dublin, Ireland. |
| 6 January 1929 | Gonxha is sent to India to begin her novitiate in Darjeeling. |
| 24 May 1931 | After two years as a novice, Gonxha takes her first vows; she takes the name Teresa. |
| 24 May 1937 | Sister Teresa takes her final vows in Loreto School, Darjeeling, India. |
| 1938–1948 | Begins teaching geography at St. Mary's High School in Calcutta, where she will also serve as principal of the school. |

| | |
|---|---|
| 10 September 1946 | Inspiration Day; while riding a train, Sister Teresa receives her call to help serve the poorest of the poor. |
| 15 August 1947 | India becomes free from British rule; three nations are formed as a result of Indian independence: India, Pakistan, and Ceylon. |
| 1948 | Sister Teresa requests permission to leave the Loreto Order to live alone and work with the poor in Calcutta; her first act is to open a school in the slum of Motijhil; on April 12, she receives permission from Pope Pius XII to remain a nun who will report directly to the archbishop of Calcutta; in August, she travels to Patna where she works with the American Medical Missionary Sisters for three months of intensive medical training; she returns to Calcutta in December; she will also become a citizen of India. |
| 1949 | Moves in with the Gomes family at 14 Creek Lane in February; in March, Subashni Das, a young Bengali girl, becomes the first to join Mother Teresa. |
| 7 October 1950 | The new congregation of the Missionaries of Charity is approved. |
| 1952 | Mother Teresa and the Missionaries of Charity move to their new motherhouse located at 54A Lower Circular Road; in August, Mother Teresa opens Nirmal Hriday, the first home for the dying, next to the temple at Kalighat. |
| 1953 | The first group of Missionaries of Charity take their first vows; Shishu Bhavan, the first home for abandoned and handicapped children, is opened. |
| 1957 | Mother Teresa begins working with lepers of Calcutta. |
| 1959 | The first houses outside of Calcutta are opened. |
| 1960 | Mother Teresa travels outside of India for the first time since coming there in 1929. |
| 1963 | The Missionaries of Charity Brothers is established. |
| 1965 | Shantinagar, the Place of Peace for Lepers, is opened. |
| 1969 | The International Association of Co-Workers of Mother Teresa becomes officially affiliated with the Missionaries of Charity. |

| 1979 | Mother Teresa is awarded the Nobel Peace Prize. |
| 1983 | Suffers heart attack while visiting in Rome. |
| 1985 | Receives Medal of Freedom from the United States, the highest civilian award given. |
| 1987 | The Missionaries of Charity establish hospices for people with AIDS. |
| 1989 | Suffers second heart attack; doctors implant pacemaker. |
| 1991 | Prepares to step down as head of Missionaries of Charity because of poor health; she is re-elected with one dissenting vote—her own. |
| 1994 | Documentary film *Hell's Angel* is broadcast on the BBC Channel Four. |
| 1996 | Granted honorary American citizenship. |
| 1997 | Sister Nirmala elected to succeed Mother Teresa as leader of Missionaries of Charity; Mother Teresa dies after having a heart attack at the Motherhouse in Calcutta. |

# Chapter 1

# SKOPJE

Located in Macedonia, in a region that was formerly part of Albania, the city of Skopje was a bustling commercial center at the beginning of the twentieth century. The city, which straddles the Vardar River, rises approximately 800 feet above sea level. The summers are long and dry, the winters damp, cold, and foggy. Not large by contemporary standards, Skopje had a population of 25,000 at the turn of the century.

Founded during the third century B.C. by the Dardanians, early descendants of modern-day Albanians from Illyna in the western Balkan Peninsula and Thracians who lived north of ancient Greece, Skopje, then known as Skupi, later came under the control of the Romanians. By the sixth century, the area fell under the domination of a Slavic people known as the Beregheziti. It was they who gave the city its current name.

By the ninth century, owing in part to the weakness of the Byzantine Empire, with its capital in Constantinople (now Istanbul in modern Turkey), Albania came under the dominion of a succession of foreign powers including the Bulgarians, Norman crusaders from France, the Angevins of southern Italy, the Venetians, and the Serbs. The Serbian occupation that began in 1347 was especially hard, prompting huge numbers of Albanians to migrate to Greece and the Aegean islands.

A few decades later the Albanians confronted a new threat. The Turks expanded their empire, known as the Ottoman Empire, to include the Balkan Peninsula. Invading Albania in 1388, the Ottoman Turks, by the middle of the fifteenth century, had succeeded in occupying the entire kingdom. The Turks may have occupied the land, but they had less success governing the Albanian people. In 1443, Gjergj Kastrioti, also known as Skenderbeg, rallied the Albanian princes and drove the Turks out. For the next 25 years, operating out of a mountain stronghold, Skenderbeg frustrated every Turkish attempt to regain Albanian territory. His brave fight against one of the mightiest powers of the time won esteem throughout the Western world, as well as securing military and financial support from the Kingdom of Naples, the papacy, Venice, and Ragusa (a province in Sicily located on the southwest side). With Skenderbeg's death in 1468, however, Albanian resistance gradually eroded, allowing the Turks to reoccupy the kingdom by 1506, again incorporating it into the Ottoman Empire. Even after his death, however, Skenderbeg's legacy of resistance strengthened Albanian solidarity, kept alive a sense of national identity, and served as a source of inspiration in the ongoing struggle for national unity and independence.

## A FORGOTTEN PEOPLE

The Turks established their dominion over Albania just as the Renaissance was beginning in Italy. Turkish domination of the Balkans cut the region off from contact and exchanges with Western Europe. As a consequence, Albania had no chance to participate in, or benefit from, the emphasis on human capabilities and accomplishments that characterized the Renaissance. Not only did the Balkans miss out on the Renaissance, but the Turks' conquest of Albania also caused great suffering and vast destruction of the economy and commerce as well as traditional art and culture. To escape persecution, about one-fourth of the Albanian population fled to southern Italy, Sicily, and the northern part of the Dalmatian coast. Countless others who remained converted to Islam, the religion of the Ottoman Empire.

Although the Turks ruled Albania for more than four hundred years, they failed to extend their authority throughout the kingdom. In the highland regions, the Turks exercised only a formal sovereignty. Beyond the reach of the government and the military, the Albanian highlanders refused to pay taxes, to serve in the army, or to surrender their weapons. They did, however, attempt to appease the Turks by offering an annual tribute to Constantinople. Even those Albanians who did fall under Turkish sway proved difficult to manage. They rose in rebellion time and again against their conquerors.

To quell Albanian resistance, which was motivated as much by the defense of Christianity as by the desire for independence, the Turks initiated a systematic effort to convert Albanians to Islam. By the end of the seventeenth century, approximately two-thirds of Albanians had embraced

Islam. Like their counterparts who had earlier converted, these men and women became Muslims not primarily from religious conviction but to escape the exploitation and violence directed toward Christians. Those who refused to convert, for example, endured a crushing tax burden from which Muslims were exempt. The so-called process of Islamization aggravated the religious fragmentation of Albanian society, which had began during the Middle Ages. The residue of this religious division persisted into the nineteenth century when leaders of the Albanian national movement used the rallying cry "the religion of Albanians is Albanianism" to overcome religious division and foster a sense of national unity.

By the middle of the nineteenth century the Ottoman Empire was weakening. Turkey, known as "The Sick Man of Europe," was having trouble maintaining its hold on its many possessions. Sensing an opportunity to break free of Ottoman domination, the Albanians, along with other Balkan peoples, sought to attain their independence. In 1878, the leaders of the Albanian independence movement met in Prizren, a town in Kosovo, to found the Albanian League of Prizren. The league had two main goals. First, to unify Albanian territory, which the Turks had split into four provinces: Kosovo, Shkodra, Monastir, and Janina. Initially, the League of Prizren advocated not Albanian independence, but the creation of an autonomous Albanian state within the Ottoman Empire. Second, the league initiated a movement to promote Albanian cultural nationalism, emphasizing a distinctly Albanian language, literature, art, and education. Although the Turks suppressed the League of Prizren in 1881, the nationalist spirit of the league lived on. Inspired by the league, Albanian leaders met in the town of Monastir in 1908 to adopt a national alphabet. Based mostly on Latin, this alphabet supplanted several others, including Arabic and Greek, then in use. It is impossible to overestimate the value of an Albanian national language to the drive for national identity and independence.

In addition to repression, however, Turkish leaders promised to reform their administration of Albania to give the Albanians greater power to determine local affairs. When in 1908, however (the same year in which the Albanians adopted a national alphabet), a group called the Young Turks, bent on modernizing and strengthening the empire, seized control of the Turkish government, they ignored previous commitments to the Albanians. Frustrated at this turn of events, Albanians took up arms and in 1912 forced the Turks, in effect, to grant Albania near independence. Alarmed at the prospect of an independent Albania, Albania's Balkan neighbors, who had already made plans to partition the region, declared war on Turkey in October 1912. To prevent the annihilation of the country, Albanian delegates met in Vlorë and, on November 28, 1912, issued the Vlorë Proclamation in which they formally declared Albanian independence. In the midst of these ethnic, national, and religious conflicts, a child was born in Skopje who would one day try to overcome these differences in order, as she said, to do God's work on earth.

## THE FAMILY

One of the most ardent nationalists in Skopje was the independent building contractor and wholesale importer of food named Nikola Bojaxhiu. The son of a large and prosperous family that had long engaged in various commercial enterprises, Bojaxhiu moved from Prizren to Skopje because of its growing reputation as a trading center. An ambitious man, Bojaxhiu quickly bought a house in Skopje and in a short time acquired a number of additional properties. Among his first ventures was supplying medicine to one of the leading doctors in town. He later went into partnership with an Italian businessman who traded in a wide variety of goods including oil, sugar, cloth, and leather.

By all accounts, Bojaxhiu was a more-than-capable businessman; he was fluent in five languages and had traveled extensively throughout Europe, the Near East, and North Africa. In addition, he was heavily involved in local politics, serving on the town council, and his contracting firm helped to build the first movie theater in Skopje. A patron of the arts, Bojaxhiu was also a faithful member of the local Roman Catholic Church.

In time, Bojaxhiu took a wife, marrying Dranafile Bernai in Prizren, the city in which the Albanian League was created and where Bojaxhiu had once lived. The couple soon returned to Skopje, settling into a spacious house with a large garden. Before long, Dranafile gave birth to three children: a daughter, Aga, was born in 1904; a son, Lazar, followed in 1907. On August 26, 1910, the couple welcomed their second daughter and last child, Agnes Gonxha. A day later, on August 27, Gonxha, which means "flower bud" in Albanian, was baptized at the local Catholic Church.

As an adult, Gonxha spoke little of her childhood, saying only that it had been pleasant. What information there is about her early life comes from her brother, Lazar, who, in describing their childhood together, also remembered it as carefree and peaceful. Although a strict disciplinarian, Nikola also took special delight in his children. Rarely did a day pass when they did not eagerly await his return home, and he often brought them trinkets as a token of his fatherly affection. Bojaxhiu also entertained his children, for he had a talent for storytelling, and recounted for them the sights he had seen and the people he had met on his travels. Then, too, the Bojaxhiu household was often crowded with the visitors who regularly stopped by to talk business or politics with Nikola.

Drana Bojaxhiu, or Nana Loke ("Mother Soul"), as the children called her, was a traditional Albanian housewife who looked after her husband and children. During the day, she cooked, cleaned, and mended clothing. As soon as Nikola returned home, though, all work stopped. Drana put on a clean dress, combed her hair, and made sure the children were presentable to greet their father.

Like her husband, Drana was a stern taskmaster and had little patience with foolish behavior. One of the few stories that Gonxha told about her early life illustrated her mother's attitude toward what she considered frivolity. One evening as the children were chattering, their conversation grew sillier. Drana listened but said nothing. At last she left the room and turned off the main electric switch, plunging the house into darkness. Gonxha concluded: "She told us that there was no use wasting electricity so that such foolishness could go on."[1] Drana passed this trait on to her youngest daughter; as an adult, Mother Teresa objected to wasted time and wasted words.

Agnes Gonxha resembled her mother in other ways. A bit plump like Drana, Agnes also had her mother's oval face and distinctive nose; she was unmistakably her mother's daughter. Her brother recalled that Gonxha was also generous and helpful, even though her behavior sometimes got her into trouble. Gonxha, for instance, helped Lazar to scale the cupboard and steal their mother's jam or desserts. Needless to say, Drana did not approve.

## FAITH AND FATHERLAND—FE Y ATDHE

All the Bojaxhiu children learned early the idea "Faith and Fatherland," or "Fe Y Atdhe." This ideal became deeply embedded in their thinking, and remained strong throughout their childhood. The strong nationalist pride of the Albanian people, personified in their father, Nikola Bojaxhiu, became a constant in their lives. Lazar remembered his father telling him and his sisters never to forget whose children they were and from what background they came. Besides opening his home to political discussion, Nikola also provided financial assistance to the cause of Albanian independence. November 28, 1912, when Gonxha was only two years old, marked a joyous day in the Bojaxhiu household. On that day the Albanians declared their independence, and Nikola and other patriots played and danced well into the night.

Nikola may have passed on to his children a sense of ethnic identity and nationalist pride; however, it was Drana who nurtured the children's spiritual growth. Almost every evening, the Bojaxhiu family gathered in the living room to recite the rosary. Drana also oversaw the children's evening prayers. A devout Catholic who went to Mass almost every day, Drana not only made sure her children practiced their religion but also incorporated it into their everyday lives. This was easier said than done. The Roman Catholic community in Albania was small; fewer than 10 percent of the population declared themselves Roman Catholic. Although few in number, the Roman Catholic community in Skopje and throughout Albania was close-knit.

Not only did Drana practice religious devotion, she also believed deeply in the spiritual value of good works. She was always available to help those in need. In this practice, her husband supported her and Gonxha aided her. On any given day, Nikola left with Drana enough money to help the poor children or adults who came to the house. Commonly, the less fortunate not only received a hand out from the Bojaxhiu family, but also took meals with them, reminding the children that the needy were also part of their larger human family. "Some of them are our relations," Drana once told her children, "but all of them are our people."[2] One of the strongest of Lazar's memories is of his mother taking in a woman stricken with a tumor and nursing her back to health. Besides taking strangers into her home, Drana visited the poor in theirs, taking them food, money, and medicine. On these occasions, Gonxha often accompanied her mother, helping her as she made her way from family to family offering both spiritual and material comfort. Drana's Christian charity offered a powerful example, helping to mold Gonxha's spiritual life and to shape her destiny.

When the time came for the children to begin school, they attended classes held in Sacred Heart Church. For four years, the Bojaxhiu children studied in the Albanian language. At the fifth year, they began to learn in Serbo-Croatian. Upon leaving the church school, the children went to public schools where all the instruction was given in Serbo-Croatian. Early on, Gonxha distinguished herself as a gifted and disciplined student.

## TRAGEDY

Nikola's participation in Albanian politics continued even after independence. When, in 1919, Albanian leaders tried to acquire Kosovo, Nikola traveled to a political gathering in Belgrade, Yugoslavia. While attending a banquet, Nikola fell seriously ill. Alarmed at her husband's condition, Drana sent Gonxha to find the parish priest. He was not at home. Growing more desperate and not knowing what to do, Gonxha went to the Skopje railway station hoping to find a priest. Luck was with her. She did locate a priest who agreed to see her father. The situation was grave. Nikola was dying. The priest arrived at his bedside in time to administer Extreme Unction, today known as the Sacrament of the Sick, which Catholics receive when they are expected to die. Just as the priest finished performing the rite, Nikola began to hemorrhage (bleed internally) and was rushed to the hospital. Emergency surgery failed to save him. Gonxha's robust and outgoing father was dead at the age of 45. The doctors and family were convinced that his political enemies had poisoned him, though no conclusive evidence ever emerged to prove the allegation.

Overnight, life in the Bojaxhiu household changed. Following Nikola's death, his partner took over the business and left nothing for the family. In addition, even though Drana had the right to estates that her family owned, she had no documents to prove her claim, nor did she have the time, inclination, energy, or money to pursue the matter through the courts. Only the family home remained.

Nikola's death devastated his wife; Drana fell into deep, prolonged, and often incapacitating grief. Responsibility for the younger children fell increasingly on the shoulders of the oldest, Aga. After several months, Drana began to emerge from her mourning. At least the family had a place to live, though Drana wondered how, with her husband's resources gone, she could provide for her children.

## "HOME IS WHERE THE MOTHER IS"

Fortunately, Drana Bojaxhiu was possessed of an entrepreneurial spirit and soon set about rebuilding her life and supporting her children. She handcrafted embroidery and was soon not only selling her handiwork, but marketing the various types of cloth and carpets for which Skopje was famous. Lazar remembered accompanying his mother to the textile factories where Drana met with the managers who sought her advice on designs and materials to boost sales.

As the family's financial status improved, the Bojaxhiu household once more became a place where the poor could come for a meal and sometimes a bed. As soon as she could, Drana again began to set aside money to help those in need and, despite her busy schedule, still found time to visit the poor. At least once a week she called on an elderly woman whose own family had abandoned her. File, a poor alcoholic woman, also benefited from Drana's care and largess. Six orphan children came to live in the house. Drana continued to impress upon her children the importance of helping the less fortunate. When you do good, she told the children, do it quietly, without calling attention to your own virtue.

Drana always found creative ways in which to instruct her children. Summoning them one day, she asked them to inspect a basket in which a number of good apples rested. She then placed a rotten apple in the basket and covered it. The following day, she had the children inspect the apples. They discovered that many of the apples, so luscious the day before, were now beginning to rot. The moral was simple but profound: it takes only one corrupt person to corrupt many others. She then reminded her children to stay clear of bad company lest they suffer the same fate as the good apples in the basket. Drana's influence on her children was extraordinary, especially after their father's death. Despite her need to work and manage a business, and despite her devotion to the poor, Drana still spent time with her children, who benefited immeasurably from her guidance. So powerful was Drana's presence that Gonxha recalled "Home is where the mother is."[3]

## FINDING THE PATH

As the children grew older, Drana insisted that they become more involved in the activities of their local parish church. Besides her mother, the Sacred Heart church exercised the most influence on young Gonxha. The church was not only important for its religious teaching, but, as a center of Albanian culture and identity, also reinforced the nationalism of the Bojaxhiu family.

Of the three children, Gonxha most readily became involved with the church. She early showed a tendency for religious devotion. When she learned to play the mandolin, it was the church to which she offered her talent. Along with her sister, Aga, Gonxha joined the choir; together the girls earned a reputation for their clear voices and frequently sang solos.

"I was only twelve years old...when I first felt the desire to become a nun," Mother Teresa recalled.[4] Much beyond that information, she revealed little about the circumstances that prompted her vocation. Throughout her life, Mother Teresa maintained that her religious experience was private. She would not discuss it. What made her calling extraordinary was that at age 12 Gonxha had never seen a nun. Yet, her desire to pursue a religious life did not come as a surprise to her mother. Of her three children, Gonxha suffered from the poorest health with a chronic cough and weak chest. Drana believed that if her youngest was not the first to die, she would be called to God in another way. Although at 12 Gonxha believed she had received her life's calling, she did nothing more about it. For the next six years, she continued her schooling and participated in church activities. There was, for the moment, no more talk about becoming a nun.

## FATHER JAMBREKOVIC

Father Franjo Jambrekovic, a young Jesuit priest of Croatian descent, arrived at the Sacred Heart parish in 1925. He was destined to exert a great influence on Gonxha. Among the many innovations that Father Jambrekovic carried out was the introduction of a parish library in which Gonxha soon passed countless hours reading. Father Jambrekovic also established the Sodality of Children of Mary, a Catholic organization for young girls that the Jesuits had created. Gonxha joined. Finally, Father Jambrekovic started a Catholic youth group that sponsored walks, parties, concerts, and other outings for the boys and girls of the parish.

Most important for Gonxha, Father Jambrekovic passed on to the members of Sacred Heart news of the missionary efforts that the Jesuits had undertaken. In 1924, he explained, a group of Yugoslav Jesuits had gone to Bengal, India. From their outpost, the missionaries wrote impassioned letters describing the horrible conditions under which the poor and the infirm lived. Father Jambrekovic read some of these letters to interested parishioners. On occasion, a missionary came to Sacred Heart to discuss the Jesuits' work in India and to solicit donations. Father Jambrekovic was enthusiastic in his support of these efforts, and spoke often about them. Gonxha assisted by pointing out to the younger children the location of India on a world map. After the arrival of Father Jambrekovic, she also became more active in the prayer groups of the sodality, which offered prayers for the success of Catholic missions. She told a cousin who was earning extra money by giving mandolin lessons to send the money to the poor in India.

The zeal with which Father Jambrekovic spoke of the Jesuit missions in India sparked a renewed sense of devotion in Gonxha. She was already immersed in church activities, singing in the choir, helping to organize parish festivals, and teaching the younger children their catechism. Her love of teaching and her deep religious fervor prompted her to consider the possibility of doing missionary work. As a young girl, she had dreamed of working with the poor of Africa. The more she heard about the missions in India, however, the more she was drawn to the possibility of working there.

By the late 1920s, Gonxha had grown into an attractive young woman, mature beyond her years. A good student, neat and clean in appearance, self-disciplined, and well organized, she had already earned a reputation in the community for her friendliness and willingness to help anyone. Like her mother, she cared for anyone in need.

But Gonxha was struggling with her decision to become a nun. A gifted writer and poet, she often carried a small notebook with her in which to record her poetry and reflections. She continued to play music with her friends and, at times, entertained thoughts of becoming a writer or a musician. Many of her friends regretted that she did not pursue these careers, for her talent was unquestioned.

Trying to decide what do to with her life, Gonxha turned to Father Jambrekovic for advice. During their discussions, she asked how one knew whether the calling to serve God was genuine. Father Jambrekovic explained that if one was truly called, that person would feel such deep joy at the decision that there could be little doubt. In later years, Mother Teresa acknowledged that there was no doubt in her mind about her decision, stating simply that God had made the choice for her.

By 1928, when she was 18, Gonxha was spending more time at the shrine of the Madonna of Letnice, located a short distance from Skopje on the slopes of Black Mountain. There she prayed for guidance. The place had a special meaning to Gonxha. Among the highlights of the parish year was the annual pilgrimage to the chapel of the Madonna. When Nikola was alive, the family often made the journey in a horse-drawn carriage, joining many others on their pilgrimage. After her husband died, Drana made the journey twice a year: once with a group and once alone and on foot. Gonxha had always looked forward to this trip, but because of her health, Drana sometimes kept her at home. It was at the Shrine of the Madonna that Gonxha sought affirmation of her decision to become a nun.

One day, after returning home from a visit to the shrine, Gonxha informed her mother that she had made up her mind to become a nun. Because of her interest in missionary work, she intended to apply to the order of the Loreto Sisters, an Irish branch of the Institute of the Blessed Virgin Mary who worked with the Jesuits in Bengal. Drana shut herself in her room. When she came out the next day, she gave her daughter her blessing, but also warned her that in choosing to become a nun, she must turn her life over to God without doubt, without fear, without hesitation, and without remorse.

By this time, Gonxha's brother, Lazar, had been away from home for several years, attending school in Austria and then later joining the newly formed Albanian army as a Second Lieutenant. When Lazar received the news of his younger sister's decision to become a nun, he wrote to her asking whether she was sure about her decision. Gonxha replied, "You think you are important because you are an officer serving a king with two million subjects. But I am serving the King of the whole world."[5]

All too soon, the time came for Gonxha to leave. She was to travel first to Paris, where the Mother Superior of the Loreto Sisters was to interview her to determine whether Gonxha was acceptable to the order. On August 15, 1928, the Feast of the Assumption, Gonxha traveled for the last time to the shrine of the Madonna of Letnice. Later, she attended a concert by the Sodality group, which was given partly to honor her, and had her photograph taken. That evening, guests came to the Bojaxhiu home to wish her farewell. Many of her friends and family brought gifts; one of those she most treasured was a gold fountain pen that a cousin gave to her.

The next day, Gonxha went to the Skopje railway station. Her mother and sister traveled with her as far as Zagreb; friends gathered to wish the Bojaxhiu women a safe journey. Gonxha cried and waved her handkerchief from the train window in farewell. The threesome made the most of their time in Zagreb. Finally, on October 8, Gonxha, accompanied by another young woman, Betika Kanjc, who also hoped to join the Loreto Sisters, boarded the train to Paris. As Gonxha made her way to the train, her mother and sister returned to Skopje. Waving goodbye, Gonxha bid farewell to her mother, whom she never saw again.

## NOTES

1. Eileen Egan, *Such a Vision of the Street: Mother Teresa—The Spirit and the Work* (New York: Image Books, 1986), p. 9.

2. Kathryn Spink, *Mother Teresa* (San Francisco: Harper & Row, 1997), pp. 6–7.

3. Spink, *Mother Teresa*, p. 6.

4. Navin Chawla, *Mother Teresa: The Authorized Biography* (Rockport, Mass.: Element, 1992), p. 3.

5. Spink, *Mother Teresa*, p. 11.

# Chapter 2

# ANSWERING THE CALL

As the train pulled away from the Zagreb station on its way to Paris, Gonxha must have thought about the consequences of her decision. Not only was she leaving family and friends, she was also leaving the only home she had ever known. If the Loreto Sisters accepted her application it would mean lifetime separation from her family and her country. She could probably never even visit her homeland again. The chances of her family visiting her were equally remote; travel was expensive and there would be little opportunity for her mother, brother, or sister to come to India. Whether she felt sad and lonely as the train rolled on toward Paris, Gonxha knew that she had made the right choice. Her life belonged to God.

## THE INSTITUTE OF THE BLESSED VIRGIN MARY

The order that Gonxha hoped to join has a long and difficult history. In 1609, an English woman named Mary Ward established the Institute of the Blessed Virgin Mary (IBVM), with which the Loreto Sisters are affiliated. Ward believed passionately in the equality of women, and determined that they should be educated accordingly. In creating the IBVM, Ward envisioned women living and acting in the world. She did not want members of the Institute to live cloistered lives, as was the tradition for Catholic women's religious orders. Rather, inspired by the Gospels, women would carry the love of Christ to those most in need of it: the poor, the downtrodden, and the helpless. Ward also saw this woman-centered order as being relatively free from the governance of male hierarchy that dominated the church.

Ward took as her model the Society of Jesus, the Jesuits. Founded in 1539 by Ignatius Loyola, a former soldier turned priest, the Jesuits were not only missionaries but teachers. Loyola believed that by offering religious and moral instruction, by making devotional life accessible to the young, and by preaching a message of service to others, the Jesuits offered the greatest service to God and His holy church.

Ward's interest in Catholic education arose in part because of the continuing religious persecution of Catholics in England after King Henry VIII broke with the church in 1534; as a result, English Catholics often fled and sought their religious education on the continent. Ward and her associates established their first school at St. Omer, France. While there, Ward and her group became known to the locals as the English Ladies, a description still applied throughout much of Western Europe. Despite facing continuous financial difficulty, Ward in time established houses and schools in Bavaria (Germany), Austria, and Italy. To communicate with these different convents, Ward traveled between countries mostly on foot.

Although successful, Ward's vision came at a price. Her ideas about women's role in religious life were so novel, especially in the Catholic world, that in 1631, church authorities suppressed the Institute. Charged with heresy, Mary was herself imprisoned by the Inquisition and briefly excommunicated, or banned, from the Roman Catholic Church. Only through the intervention of Pope Urban VIII was she eventually freed and reinstated to full church membership, her organization now operating under papal protection.

In 1639, Ward returned to England where the climate toward Catholics had improved during the reign of King Charles I, who had married a Catholic princess and was himself sympathetic to Catholicism. Ward remained in England until she died in Yorkshire in 1645. Upon her death, the Institute was in shambles. Embroiled in a civil war against his political and religious enemies—a war he was destined to lose, and with it his kingdom and his head—Charles could offer the order scant protection. Radical English Protestants, known as the Puritans, who prevailed in the civil war against Charles, disbanded Ward's houses and schools in England. In 1650, the year after Puritan leaders had executed Charles, the Sisters of the Blessed Virgin Mary again fled England, seeking refuge in Catholic France. Not until 1677 did they return to Yorkshire under the protection of Charles II, the son of Charles I who had been restored to the throne in 1660. Like his father, Charles II was sympathetic to Catholicism. It was only through the perseverance of Ward's followers, and the protection that both the Vatican and the English crown extended, that the IBVM survived to continue the work that she had inspired.

## THE LORETO SISTERS

Recognizing the need for Catholic education in their homeland, Irish church officials invited the IBVM sisters to establish a school in Dublin. However, the Institute was not in a position to send Sisters immediately, but arranged that a young local woman, Frances Ball, would join the organization and recruit other Irish women. In 1814, Ball traveled to York, returning to Dublin in 1821. Now known as Mother Teresa, Ball settled at Rathfarnham House with two companions. Because the three women lived together in Rathfarnham House, Mother Teresa decided to call their order "Loreto" after the Italian village to which the home of the Holy Family (Jesus, Mary, and Joseph) was supposed to have been miraculously transported. The name stuck, and eventually the order became known as "Loreto Sisters," although the official title remains the Institute of the Blessed Virgin Mary.

Early in 1841, a German missionary asked Mother Teresa to send members of her order to India. By then, generations of Irish, having enlisted in the British Army, were stationed in India, which was part of the British Empire. Many had married and started families. If, however, one or another of the parents died or if they deserted their family, scores of Irish children were lost to the Catholic Church. Beginning in 1834, the Jesuits began arriving in Bengal near Calcutta to deal with this problem. They established St. Xavier's School in which they taught Catholics, Hindus, and Muslims alike. It soon became apparent, though, that the community needed a separate school for the daughters of Irish Catholic military families.

When first approached about the possibility of sending nuns to India to staff the girls school, Mother Teresa gently but firmly refused. There were too many children in Ireland in need of assistance. There was also a shortage of nuns. Her German visitor countered that in refusing to send members of her order to India, Mother Teresa was, in effect, refusing to provide a Christian education for those children. Mother Teresa relented. The priest could make his case before the entire community; they would decide whether to accept the mission to India.

In the end, seven sisters decided to go to India, marking the beginning of Loreto missionary work there. On August 23, 1841, the seven, accompanied by two priests and six postulants, or novice nuns, set sail. Almost four months later, they disembarked in Calcutta. The little band took possession of the house at 5 Middleton Row, where they were to live and teach. The sisters prepared the once lavishly furnished house into simpler living quarters and classrooms. The 67-foot dining room became the school hall.

The sisters then traveled to the local orphanage near the cathedral of Our Lady of the Rosary to meet with church officials and the children. Finally, on January 10, 1842, the Loreto School opened its doors to boarders and day students. As became the custom with the Loreto Sisters, students whose families could afford to do so paid tuition. Their monies, combined with other donations, enabled the sisters to provide a free education for children of the poor and to operate an orphanage and a widow's asylum.

The initial reports that Mother Teresa received from India were enthusiastic. Streams of volunteers now offered to go to India to aid the Loreto Sisters of Calcutta. Even when a number of the nuns died of cholera, the flow of volunteers did not stop. It was this pioneering and courageous group of teachers that Gonxha Bojaxhiu soon hoped to join.

## RATHFARNHAM HOUSE

Upon their arrival in Paris, the two girls were taken to the Villa Molitor to see Mother Eugene MacAvin, the sister in charge of the Loreto House in Paris. There they were interviewed with the help of an interpreter from the Yugoslavian embassy. Both Gonxha and Betike were approved and then sent on to Dublin where they would stay at the Loreto Abbey at Rathfarnham House.

The two arrived at Rathfarnham, a simple red-brick building, in September; Gonxha was somewhat comforted upon seeing the statue of the Blessed Mother in the courtyard. The two young women, wearing the long white habit, or dress, and black veil of the Loreto nuns, spent most of the next six weeks studying English, the language in which they were to teach. In order to help them become more comfortable with the language, the two were instructed never to speak in their native tongue, something that both Betike and Gonxha obediently followed. Unlike the native-speaking novitiates, Gonxha and Betike received little other instruction and had little opportunity to get to know many of the other sisters and postulates staying at Loreto Abbey. From all accounts, though, it appeared that Gonxha had inherited her father's flair for languages and was further helped in her studies by Mother Mary Emmanuel McDermott who was another postulant at Loreto Abbey. At the end of six weeks, on December 1, 1928, the two women set sail for India and their new life. Upon their arrival there, the two would begin their novitiate, that is the period of study and prayer which every nun takes before her final vows.

The sea voyage proved long and arduous, winding its way through the Suez Canal, then the Red Sea, the Indian Ocean, and finally the Bay of

Bengal. Christmas was celebrated aboard the ship with three other Franciscan nuns, also missionaries bound for India. The group sang Christmas carols around a small paper crib made quickly for the celebration. Their only regret was that there was no priest aboard to celebrate mass. But that all changed when the ship made port at Colombo, where a priest would accompany the nuns for the rest of the voyage.

On January 6, 1929, the ship made port at Calcutta. But at this point, Gonxha had little chance to become acquainted with her surroundings. After just a few days, on January 16, she was sent to the Loreto Novitiate located in Darjeeling, a fashionable hill resort about 400 miles north of Calcutta.

## LIFE IN THE LORETO CONVENT

Life at the Loreto Convent for Gonxha Bojaxhiu was disciplined and rigorous. Entering a Catholic convent during the early twentieth century was like being plunged into another world, one that was isolated and relatively contained. For the next two years, dressed in the black habit and veil of the order, Gonxha kept up with her English studies as well as learning the Bengali language. Under the watchful eye of the novice mistress, who oversaw the novitiates' training, the young women went weekly to confession. Dinnertime was spent listing to one of the sisters reading about the lives of the saints, or from the rules of Loreto. Every day from 9 to 11, Gonxha and the other novitiates taught at St. Teresa's School, a one-room schoolhouse affiliated with the convent. Here 20 small boys and girls met to receive instruction. She quickly earned a reputation for being hard working, cheerful, and charitable in her dealings with others.

On March 24, 1931, Gonxha Bojaxhiu took her first vows—a lifetime promised to chastity, poverty, and obedience to God as a sister of Loreto. As was the custom, Gonxha had chosen a new name for herself to symbolize her new life with God. Her choice was an inspired one based on the late-nineteenth-century French nun Thérèse Martin who received her call to serve Christ at a young age and was especially interested in missionary work. She entered the Carmelite order at the age of 15, and throughout her life, Thérèse dedicated her prayers and service toward missionaries and their success. She hoped one day to become a missionary herself to serve with the Carmelite convent in Hanoi, Indochina (now Vietnam). Unfortunately, her dream was never realized, as she was struck down by tuberculosis at the age of 24.

Throughout her short life, Thérèse Martin strove to honor God in what she called her "little way," that is a life given to the Lord in complete trust and self-surrender, much like a child with a loving parent. In 1927, Pope Pius XI canonized Thérèse Martin who now became St. Thérèse of the Child Jesus, and the patron saint of missions. In light of Gonxha's own life, her choice came as no surprise.

Unfortunately, there was a problem with her choice. There was already one nun in the convent with the name Marie-Thérèse. Not wanting to change her chosen name, Gonxha merely decided to go by the Spanish spelling "Teresa." Still the name change caused some confusion throughout her life, as she was thought to have taken the name of the great Spanish saint, Teresa of Avila. Whenever asked, however, she always patiently explained her choice. For the sisters in the Loreto Convent, however, the new Teresa soon had a nickname that further distinguished her: Bengali Teresa, an acknowledgment of her ability to speak the language so well.

## BENGALI TERESA

Not long after taking her vows, Gonxha Bojaxhiu, now called Sister Teresa, took the train from Darjeeling to Calcutta. There, she was to begin teaching at St. Mary's School, located in the eastern district of Calcutta. It was to be her place of residence and work for the next 17 years.

During the 1920s, the contrast between the cities of Darjeeling and Calcutta was startling. In Darjeeling, one breathed clear mountain air, and a walk in a flower-filled meadow was not far away. It was a city of refined culture, of modern European architecture and imported luxury, a retreat for those unaccustomed to the heat and humidity of India. Calcutta, while a dynamic and cosmopolitan city, serving as the political capital of British India, was another story. The city teemed with humanity, overcrowded and spilling into the streets and alleys throughout. It was on one hand a city enriched by the culture and arts of India; on the other, it was a cesspool of human misery and degradation.

Upon her arrival, Sister Teresa was taken to the eastern district of the city where the school and living quarters for the Loreto nuns was located. Here the Loreto Sisters worked with the Daughters of Saint Anne, a local congregation of nuns founded by the Loreto Sisters in 1898. These nuns, who were Bengali women, wore not the long black habit and veil of the European order, but the traditional sari, the dress worn by Indian women. For the hot summers, the sari worn was white; blue was used for the cooler autumn and winter months.

## ST. MARY'S SCHOOL

The school was hidden from the everyday world by high gray walls and tall iron gates. Upon passing through the entrance gates, one came upon a complex of buildings with playing fields and well-tended lawns. The campus comprised several buildings of varying architectural styles. Besides an administrative building and smaller gray classroom building was St. Mary's School. There were also quarters for the nuns and for those students who boarded at the school, mostly orphans, girls from broken homes, and children with only one parent.

The school had already established a reputation for itself. Established in 1841, as one of the six Loreto schools in Calcutta, the Calcutta school in Entally educated orphans, the sons and daughters of the affluent and foreign families living in the city. All children wore the same uniform; there was no distinction by the sisters of the rich from the poor, the European from the Indian, Catholic from non-Catholic. The school was also known for educating "Loreto Girls," that is young Indian women who graduated from Loreto College and who would go on to positions in education and social welfare within Calcutta and India. Not only did teachers and welfare workers graduate from Loreto College, but in time the first woman judge of the Delhi High Court, a judge of the High Court of Calcutta, and several members of the Indian Parliament all received degrees from Loreto. In all, some 500 children and young women were in attendance at the Loreto schools at Entally.

Here Sister Teresa took her place, teaching alongside the Daughters of St. Anne. She taught history and geography. She also became more comfortable in her use of the Bengali language as St. Mary's classes were taught in both English and Bengali. She soon added another language, Hindi. Her classrooms varied: sometimes, she taught in what once had been a chapel and was now broken into five class areas; other times, she taught in what was once the stables, or outside in the courtyard.

Though the Loreto Sisters might have been sequestered behind the walls of their school and convent, they were not sheltered from the overwhelming poverty of the area; for the poor conditions of the area were found in the shabby environment of the school itself. Everyday, before beginning the day's lessons, Sister Teresa rolled up the sleeves of her habit, found water and a broom, and proceeded to sweep the floor, much to the delight and amazement of her students, as only people of the very lowest caste performed menial duties such as these. When Teresa saw where the children ate and slept, she was distressed at the terrible condition there.

Yet, she also found solace and comfort through the happiness and gratitude of her young charges. Merely placing a hand on a dirty forehead or holding the hand of a small child brought her great joy. Many of the children took to calling her "Ma" which meant "Mother," a term that she treasured.

According to one former student, among the tasks Sister Teresa willingly took on was the organization of classes for the primary school children. Sister Teresa also made sure that the children received baths; for many, this was a real treat and something to look forward to. Prizes were awarded at the end of the school year for the students; in many cases, the most coveted were bars of soap.

Former students remember Sister Teresa as an engaging teacher. When teaching Sunday School catechism lessons, she often told stories of her own childhood in Skopje. Her geography classes were exciting; many students believed that she made the world come alive for them in a way not seen or felt before. This is, perhaps, ironic because Sister Teresa had seen little of the world herself and would not leave the area she resided in for over 30 years.

By all accounts, Sister Teresa again showed her willingness to work hard. She needed her fortitude; the days at St. Mary's were long. Each day began at half past five in the morning. Upon awakening, the sisters would pray and read their prescribed lessons in the prayer book, or from the Scriptures or New Testament. All were expected to attend morning mass at six o'clock. Classes were held from 9 A.M. to 3 P.M., with tea held afterward. Other hours at St. Mary's were used for looking after the small children there. There were also other duties awaiting them: papers and lessons to be corrected and a children's recreation hour to be supervised. Sister Teresa also oversaw the children's evening meals and bedtime. Self-discipline was essential if one was to accomplish everything in a timely fashion. Failure to do so indicated an inability to stay within the order.

Throughout her time at the school, Sister Teresa showed herself to be a pious but not overly demonstrative woman. She was charitable and did not tolerate unkindness from anyone, whether a child or an adult. Taking a firm attitude toward her young charges, Sister Teresa rarely displayed her temper at wrongdoing. In spite of the backbreaking work, she always had a smile and a kind word for people. She was no stranger to humor either: when told a good joke or funny story, Sister Teresa clasped her waist in both hands and would often bend over with laughter.

Although the sisters of Loreto took vows to live in poverty, Sister Teresa somehow managed to acquire those things that no one else wanted. Her sheets had more patches and darns than the others. She often wore ill-fitting second-hand shoes, which over time would misshape and deform her feet. Yet she never complained, maintaining a humble and steady demeanor. She was, by all appearances, an ordinary nun, carrying out her religious duties. Neither was she particularly intelligent: her education at best was adequate. Some at the convent remember her more for her inability to light the candles at the Benediction service. As one sister who lived with her during this period recalled, "She was very ordinary. We just looked upon her as one of our Sisters who was very devoted and dedicated."[1] It was this very ordinariness that made the journey Sister Teresa embarked upon so extraordinary.

Sister Teresa also helped with the Sodality of the Blessed Virgin, the same organization that had so heavily influenced her life in Skopje. Working with Father Julien Henry, a Belgian Jesuit priest, Sister Teresa participated in the meetings, prayers, and study club sponsored by the group. In addition, Sister Teresa, working with Father Henry, helped the girls of sodality aid the poor.

On the other side of the convent wall was the slum area (*bustee*) known as Motijhil, or Pearl Lake, named for a discolored sump-water pond located in the center of the area. It was from this pond that the residents drew their drinking, cooking, and washing water. Surrounding the pond were the wretched, mud-floor huts of the poor who lived in the neighborhood. It was an area desperately in need of comfort. For Father Henry, this was an opportunity to teach the older girls of St. Mary's about works of service. Every day during the school week, the priest met with the girls whose ages ranged from the early teens to their early twenties.

On Saturday, the girls left the walls of their compound and ventured into Motijhil in groups to visit with these families, often bearing small items for the children of the poor. Other groups traveled to the Nilratan Sarkar Hospital to visit the sick, where they comforted family members or wrote letters for those unable to do so. Although Sister Teresa took great stock in the efforts of her students, she could not join them because of the rule of enclosure practiced by the Loreto nuns. But perhaps the most important outcome of these efforts was the indirect link forged between the poor of Calcutta and Sister Teresa.

On May 24, 1937, Sister Teresa traveled to Darjeeling to take her final vows. During the ceremony, Teresa solemnly committed herself to the Loreto Sisters and to a lifetime of poverty, chastity, and obedience in service to the Lord. Upon her return to Calcutta, she once again plunged into her busy days and teaching, much to the delight of several young children who feared that she had gone away for good. Nothing had changed, save Sister Teresa's name. She was now to be addressed as

Mother Teresa, the name she would go by for the rest of her life. At the age of 27, her destiny seemed to be fulfilled. At the same time, India was in the midst of trying to fulfill its own destiny.

## THE JEWEL IN THE CROWN

The India that Mother Teresa came to was no longer the bright and glittering jewel in the British Empire's crown. By 1929, the British had been in India for a little over three centuries and had governed it exclusively for over 70 years. Now in the early years of the twentieth century, a growing unrest among Indian natives for self-government was increasing and British control over its largest colony was waning.

The British presence in India is a long and dramatic story. Beginning in the late fifteenth century with the early sea voyages of Portuguese explorer Vasco da Gama, India became a prized possession eagerly sought by many European countries. The Portuguese were the first to claim India, her people, and her natural resources for their own. Over the next two centuries, the Dutch, British, and French challenged the Portuguese for the Indian trade.

Of all the European nations to lay claim to India, Britain eventually won and stayed. Beginning in 1600, with the creation of the British East India Company, the British established trading posts in the key cities of Madras, Bombay, and Calcutta. Despite an encroaching French presence, the English held fast. By 1757, the British had established a strong foothold in the country.

What began as a trading empire gradually grew into political rule. That the conquest came about as the result of a private trading company engaging in conflict chiefly through the use of native Indian soldiers, known as Sepoys, seemed to matter little. By 1849, the rule of the British East India Company was extended over virtually the whole of the subcontinent by conquest or treaties.

Despite the use of natives as soldiers, the British took a rather high-handed approach to their new possession. Missionaries introduced Christianity and English customs, but not all Indians were eager to give up their traditional ways. As a result, a great wave of unrest began building, and exploded in 1857, when a rumor was circulated among the company's Indian soldiers that the rifle cartridge-papers they had to tear with their teeth were greased with the fat of cows and pigs. The cow is sacred to Hindus, and the pig is abhorred by Muslims. The rumor provoked the great Sepoy Revolt, or Indian Mutiny, of 1857 in which hundreds of British were killed. By the time the mutiny was quelled, the East India Company no longer controlled British India, and a year later, the British Crown took over the administration. Almost two decades later, in 1876, Parliament ruled that India should be designated part of the British empire; the following year Queen Victoria was crowned empress of India.

## THE BRITISH RAJ

For the next quarter century following the Indian Mutiny, British rule, or raj, of India was at its peak. Haunted by the horrific memory of the mutiny, the British government enacted a series of measures to avoid another conflict from taking place. To oversee the day-to-day administration of the colony's provinces, a viceroy of India was appointed by the crown. However, Hindu and Muslim princes continued to govern almost 600 native states, which were for the most part autonomous. However, they were forbidden to make war on one another, and to keep an eye on things, the viceroy appointed an agent to each royal state whose job it was to advise the ruler.

British rule brought internal peace and economic development to India. The British not only built roads and railways, but canals, irrigation works, mills, and factories. They introduced Western law and police systems, modernized cities, and built schools. Despite these efforts at nation building, many Indians resented the aloof and exacting attitude of the British government. A growing number of Indian intellectuals, many of whom were the products of an English education, began dreaming of a free India. In 1885, the Indian National Congress was created; its establishment marked the beginnings of a growing and organized protest for Indian independence.

## TOWARD A FREE INDIA

At the outbreak of World War I in 1914, Indian troops were called upon to aid the British and their allies against the Germans. Although Indians did so, in the wake of the war, nationalist agitation increased. The British Parliament, recognizing that something had to be done to appease the nationalists, passed a reform act in 1919, which provided for the creation of provincial councils that allowed Indians to participate in helping form policy with regard to agriculture, education, and public health. But the provincial councils were not enough for the extreme nationalists, such as those under the leadership of Mohandas K. Gandhi. This group soon gained control of the Indian National Congress. In addition, Gandhi preached resistance to the British by *noncooperation*, or nonviolent resistance in most every aspect of daily life. This meant boycotting all British-made goods, refusing to send children to British schools and colleges, ignoring British courts of law, and rejecting British titles and honors. Noncompliance extended to British elections and the British tax system. By withdrawing their support, the Indian people hoped to stop completely the British in India and allow for the creation of an independent Indian nation. Hundreds of thousands responded to Gandhi's plea and joined his civil disobedience campaigns, and the Indian National Congress quickly gained a mass following.

The situation in India was a powder keg waiting to explode. In 1927, rioting broke out when the British Parliament placed no Indians on a commission created to investigate the government of India. Soon after, the British imprisoned Gandhi and his associates but could not silence their message. In 1929, Jawaharlal Nehru was elected president of the Congress. Like Gandhi, Nehru was passionately devoted to the cause of independence. Finally in 1935, the British Parliament passed the Government of India Act, which provided for elected legislatures in the provinces, but restricted the number of eligible voters based on property and educational requirements. Amid this growing agitation between the British colonial government and Indian peoples, Mother Teresa arrived to do her work.

## THE SECOND WORLD WAR

Nonviolent resistance to the British in India continued to grow. By 1939, anti-British feelings intensified as the Indian people watched Britain once more plunge into hostilities with the Germans. The Parliament, as it had during World War I, declared a state of war with Germany on behalf of the Indian people without consulting them.

The consequences of British actions were horrendous in India, resulting in the Great Famine of 1942–1943. The transportation system was now taken over by the British military; even the small river crafts used to deliver rice to Calcutta from the paddies of Bengal were pressed into service. Burmese rice, which accounted for 10 percent of the staple food for Bengal, was cut off, causing a shortage. The Indian government, preoccupied by the war, saw the problem as one that needed to be solved locally.

Prices started to rise and both black marketers and money lenders prospered. Poor families in the rural areas, depleted of their meager savings, sold their land. With no food to eat, thousands fled the region for Calcutta, flocking to the city's already overburdened soup kitchens. Housing for the poor was already overstretched, and thousands of people died in the streets everyday. Adding to the overcrowding and chaos were the swarms of refuges fleeing the Japanese. The noise of the streets was silenced only when people sought shelter from Japanese bombs. In the end, the Great Famine claimed the lives of at least two million, though some figures put the number of deaths closer to four or five million. The death toll was so high, that the traditional funeral pyres lit for the dead, known as *ghats,* never stopped burning in some areas.

The nuns at Entally felt the war's effects, too. The number of war babies or small infants left at the doorsteps of Loreto multiplied. At one point, Mother Teresa was faced with the problem of how to feed 24 babies by bottle. Orphans fleeing the Japanese came to the convent and school looking for refuge. The convent also opened its doors to other Catholic missionaries escaping from the Japanese.

In time, the British requisitioned the Entally convent and school as a British military hospital; the dormitories, which once housed orphans, were now taken over by sick, wounded, and dying British soldiers. The Sisters of Loreto evacuated, taking with them their students and other orphans, and relocated to hotels in Darjeeling, Shillong, and Lucknow. Mother Teresa stayed in Calcutta in a building located on Convent Road. There she continued to teach and care for her young charges.

## A CLOSE COMPANION

In 1937, Mother Teresa had taken on more responsibilities; she was put in charge of the St. Teresa's Primary School as well as Sunday school classes for the children. During the war, she also took on the responsibilities of headmistress when Mother du Cenacle became ill in 1944. That she stayed in the city during the war made a tremendous impact on her students, for it was Mother Teresa's wish that the lives of the children not be any more disrupted than necessary. The school may have been moved to a different location for the time being, but Mother Teresa worked to make sure that the children's daily routine stayed as intact as possible.

It was during this period that Mother Teresa met a man who would serve as her spiritual advisor and companion for the next 45 years. Father Celeste Van Exem was a Belgian Jesuit who came to India in 1944. An expert in Arabic and the Muslim faith, he came to Calcutta with the specific intention of working with the city's Muslims. On July 11, 1944, he and two other priests moved into a house in Baithakana, located not far from Mother Teresa's small community on Convent Road. When asked whether he would celebrate Mass for Mother Teresa, Father Van Exem recalled how he initially refused, stating that he was "called to India to work for the Muslims and not for Sisters. I was a young priest who wanted to work with intellectuals; I did not want to be busy with nuns."[2]

The following day, though, Father Van Exem met with Mother Teresa. His initial impression was of a very simple nun, concerned with the plight of the poor, but for the most part unremarkable. However, Mother Teresa came away with a much higher opinion of the priest, for not long after, she asked him to become her spiritual advisor. Again, Father Van Exem demurred, saying that he had no desire to become a nun's spiritual father and that he considered the request a diversion from what he believed to be his true reason for being in Calcutta. But he told Mother Teresa that she needed to put her request in writing to the archbishop of the city. The archbishop granted Mother Teresa's request. In obedience to the bishop, Father Van Exem reluctantly assumed the role of Mother Teresa's spiritual father and director. She would turn to him often for spiritual advice and direction.

## WAR'S END AND TROUBLED TIMES

By 1945, the war ended and Mother Teresa and her charges moved back to the convent at Entally. During this period, Mother Teresa had written home to her mother describing her life in Calcutta. By now, Drana had moved to Tirana, Albania, where both Aga and Lazar lived. Drana reminded her daughter that she went to India to work with the poor; Drana also asked her daughter to recall the woman whom Drana had taken in, when no one else would. Perhaps this advice spurred Mother Teresa to rethink her duties in the convent.

No sooner had the hostilities ended with Japan, when India and Calcutta were once more plunged into hostilities and bloodshed. The Indian National Congress had been busy making preparations for India's eventual independence from British rule. Working with the Congress was the Muslim League, under the leadership of Mohammed Ali Jinnah, a lawyer. The League was pressing the Congress for the establishment of a separate homeland for India's Muslims to be called Pakistan. The new country was to be formed from a partition of India.

On August 16, 1946, the Muslim League called a meeting—what members referred to as Direct Action Day—in Calcutta in the Maidan. The speeches given by league members inflamed an already passionate crowd. As a result, for the next four nights, the city was the scene of bloody riots between Hindus and Muslims. Life came to a grinding halt as the city was pitched into terror. Militants set fire to shops with people still inside. Sewers were filled with the bodies of the dead. Men, women and children, cut by the deadly blades of knives, were left in the streets to bleed to death. Entrails spilled onto sidewalks already red with blood; most everywhere one looked there were dead bodies, while vultures circled overhead. By the end, at least 5,000 persons had perished and another 15,000 were wounded.

For Mother Teresa and the children, the riots also meant no food deliveries. Faced with the prospect of her 300 students going hungry, Mother Teresa broke one of the cardinal rules of the order: she left the convent and went into the streets alone to search for food. Years later, Mother Teresa described the scene:

> I went out from St. Mary's Entally. I had three hundred girls in the boarding school and nothing to eat. We were not supposed to go out into the streets, but I went anyway. Then I saw the bodies on the streets, stabbed, beaten, lying there in strange positions in their dried blood.... A lorry [truck full] of soldiers stopped me and told me that I should not be out on the street.... I told them that I had to come out and take the risk. I had three hundred children with nothing to eat. The soldiers had rice and they drove me back to the school and unloaded bags of rice.[3]

In the aftermath of the riots, Mother Teresa became weak and ill and was directed to rest every afternoon for three hours. Her superiors feared that her condition might make her susceptible to tuberculosis, a malady that claimed many nuns in Calcutta. Father Van Exem remembered this period as the only time he ever saw his spiritual charge cry, frustrated at her weak condition and inability to carry out her duties.

Finally it was decided that Mother Teresa needed a spiritual renewal and a physical reprieve from the work at the convent and school. She was ordered to travel to the convent in Darjeeling for a retreat, which would allow her to rest and meditate. On September 10, 1946, a day that is now celebrated annually by the Missionaries of Charity as Inspiration Day, while traveling to Darjeeling on a dusty, noisy train, Mother Teresa experienced another call. Later she would have little to say about the experience, much as she did when she first received her calling to become a nun. But to one writer, many years later, she offered her memories of that train ride: "It was on the tenth of September 1946, in the train that took me to Darjeeling,... that I heard the call of God. The message was quite clear: I was to leave the convent and help the poor while living among them."[4] Many years later she also stated that the call was quite clear, "It was an order. To fail it would have been to break the faith."[5]

## NOTES

1. Navin Chawla, *Mother Teresa: The Authorized Biography* (Rockport, Mass.: Element, 1992), p. 15.

2. Kathryn Spink, *Mother Teresa: A Complete Authorized Biography* (San Francisco: Harper & Row, 1997), p. 20.

3. Eileen Egan, *Such a Vision of the Street: Mother Teresa—The Spirit and the Work* (Garden City, N.Y.: Image Books, 1986), pp. 27–28.

4. Edward Le Joly, *Mother Teresa of Calcutta: A Biography* (San Francisco: Harper & Row, 1977), p. 9.

5. Spink, *Mother Teresa*, p. 22.

# Chapter 3

# A NEW DIRECTION AND A NEW JOURNEY

Few would disagree that Inspiration Day was a turning point for Mother Teresa. But there have been accounts of her life that have made erroneous connections between her desire to leave Loreto and her calling on the train to Darjeeling. One popular story stated that the killings and carnage she viewed during the August 1946 riots were the sole inspiration for her leaving. Another account incorrectly stated that she could view the slums of Calcutta from her bedroom window, which led to her decision.

Mother Teresa was no stranger to the poverty in Calcutta. She had seen it firsthand upon her arrival as a novitiate and later as a teacher instructing the children of the poor. But until her train ride to Darjeeling, Mother Teresa firmly believed that she was carrying out God's plan for her life and that she would best serve God as a nun living in Loreto. That was now all about to change.

## THE FIRST STEPS

As Mother Teresa recalled "The message was clear, I knew where I belonged, but I did not know how to get there."[1] On her return from Darjeeling, she immediately sought out Father Van Exem, showing him two sheets of paper on which she had written down her plans. Upon returning to his room at Baithakana, Father Van Exem placed the pieces of paper underneath a picture of the Immaculate Heart of Mary, which Mother Teresa had given to him as a Christmas gift. Two hours later, he returned and read the papers. He found the key ingredients as to what she was supposed to do: she was to leave Loreto, but she was to keep her vows. She was to start a new congregation or order of nuns, who would work for the poor in the slums. The members of this new congregation would have to take a special vow of charity for the poor. There were to be no institutions, hospitals, or clinics to help in this endeavor. Mother Teresa and her nuns were to work and live among the poorest of the poor. Special attention, too, was to be focused on those people who had no family or were unwanted in any way.

Father Van Exem did not even question Mother Teresa's explanation. Years later, he stated that he believed her new vocation was just as true as her decision to leave Skopje and become a nun. To answer this latest calling, it did not matter to Mother Teresa that she had already made one sacrifice in leaving her mother. Now she was fully prepared to make a second: leaving the safe confines of the convent at Loreto and venturing out into the streets of Calcutta to work with the poor.

When Mother Teresa returned to Loreto in October, she led a retreat in which the seeds of her new venture began to sprout. Drawing on the story of Jesus on the cross crying, "I thirst," Mother Teresa put forth the basic tenets that would guide her journey: "to quench the infinite thirst of Jesus Christ on the Cross for love of souls."[2] The importance of this idea was so great that as her organization grew and built chapels, each one would be inscribed with the two words: "I thirst." In creating the Missionaries of Charity, she expected those chosen not only to take vows of chastity, poverty, and obedience, but to take an additional vow as well: to offer themselves to the poorest of the poor.

Leaving the convent was not easy for Mother Teresa. It was, she admitted years later, the most difficult thing she had ever done, even harder than leaving her family and homeland. Besides the emotional turmoil, she still needed permission to leave. Upon consulting Father Van Exem, Mother Teresa decided to pray about her decision for a few months. In January 1947, Mother Teresa decided to write to Archbishop Ferdinand Périer about her plans; Father Van Exem would follow up with a visit.

If Father Van Exem thought that the archbishop would readily agree to Mother Teresa's plans, he was mistaken. Years later, Périer described the first time he learned of Mother Teresa:

> One day, as I was making the visit of the Entally convent, someone told me that a young nun of the Community had some queer ideas. Now, whenever anyone tried to put me on my guard in this way, I always asked my self whether the hand of God might not be there, and gave full freedom to the person

to explain his or her case. If the religious is humble, obedient, dutiful the impulse may come from God.[3]

Despite his open-mindedness, Archbishop Périer was not only against the idea of a lone nun living among the poor on the Calcutta streets, but he was also alarmed that one of his priests was apparently treating the idea with some seriousness. Soon after his meeting with Van Exem, the Archbishop ordered Mother Teresa transferred to Asansol, a city located about 175 miles northwest of Calcutta. Here, she was to maintain the kitchen as well as the garden; she would also continue teaching geography. Father Van Exem then cautioned Mother Teresa to say nothing more of her plans for the time being. The two kept up regular correspondence by mail.

## A RELUCTANT APPROVAL

While Mother Teresa was away from Entally, Archbishop Périer made several inquiries about her. Keeping her identity a secret, he spoke with Father Julien Henry of St. Teresa's Church, who also served as the pastor of St. Mary's Church in Darjeeling and was a teacher of theology. The archbishop carefully asked Father Henry what he thought of a European woman dressed in the traditional sari of Bengali women, working among the poor and dying in the city. The two also discussed whether she could succeed and if such a new order would draw in young women to serve. Then there were political questions to be considered: what would the reaction of the public be to such an idea, when already there were individuals trying to help the poor?

Father Henry believed that the archbishop's proposal was, in theory, possible. At the very least, it was a gamble, but Father Henry told the archbishop it was a gamble worth taking. Excited at the prospect of something being done for the poor of Calcutta, Father Henry even asked his congregation to pray for the success of such a program. But little did he or anyone else realize that the person behind this idea was Mother Teresa. The archbishop was not finished. In addition to speaking with Father Henry, the archbishop sought the advice of the father general of the Society of Jesus (the Jesuit Order), who in turn asked the provincial in India for his thoughts. The archbishop also sought counsel from a specialist in church law.

There was another difficulty to be considered as well. The Vatican did not look favorably on the unnecessary growth of religious vocations for women. As it was, there were already too many small orders of nuns. A bishop applying for a new congregation had to demonstrate that the existing orders did not do the work for which the new one was being established. In Calcutta, the order of the Daughters of St. Anne, with whom Mother Teresa had worked while at the Loreto school, already ministered among the poor. They also dressed in Indian style, slept in a dormitory, ate simple food, and spoke Bengali. How would Mother Teresa's new congregation be different?

The archbishop asked Mother Teresa if she could work with the Daughters of St. Anne. Mother Teresa did not think so. The Daughters had their own way of doing things and their own traditions. What Mother Teresa was proposing was quite different. Her congregation would be more mobile; they would visit the poor where needed. And she did not want just to work among the poor; she made it clear that she intended to work among the "poorest of the poor."[4] She also wanted to start from scratch and train her novices in her own way.

An entire year passed before the archbishop was satisfied with the information he had received. Only then did he give permission to Mother Teresa to write to the mother general of the Loreto Sisters, asking for permission to be released from the Order. In the letter that Father Van Exem typed for her, Mother Teresa explained her reasons for seeking her release: she wished to continue her vocation among the poor. In asking the mother superior to leave, Mother Teresa requested *exclaustration*, which simply meant that she would continue to live by her vows but would serve as a Loreto Sister in a new setting.

However, when the archbishop read the letter, he insisted that Mother Teresa change *exclaustration* to *secularization*. To be secularized meant that Mother Teresa would no longer be a member of the Loreto Order, but she would continue to honor her vows as a nun. Having to leave the Loreto Order was a severe disappointment, but as Archbishop Périer explained, she was to trust God fully and send the letter.

With a heavy heart, Mother Teresa posted the letter to the mother general in Rathfarnham in early January 1948. Less than a month later, she had her reply:

> Since this is manifestly the will of God, I hereby give you permission to write to the Congregation in Rome and for the indult. Do not speak to the Provincial. Do not speak to your Superiors. Speak to nobody. I did not speak to my own counselors. My consent is sufficient. However, do not ask for the indult of secularization, ask for the indult of exclaustration.[5]

The mother general could not have sent stronger support. Both Mother Teresa and Father Van Exem were overjoyed with the response. Mother Teresa now wrote another letter, this time to the office of the Vatican in Rome. Although the mother general told her to consult no one, Mother Teresa again gave the letter to Father Van Exem, who in turn gave it to Archbishop Périer. The archbishop again stipulated that if the letter was to be sent to Rome, Mother Teresa include her request for secularization. Despite her fears about having to leave her religious order, Mother Teresa was more worried about how to write to a cardinal. She asked Father Van Exem for help; he simply replied that a "Dear Father" would suffice and not to worry about titles, but to state her case clearly and simply. Finally in February 1948, she sent the letter to Rome. In addition to Mother Teresa's request, Archbishop Périer also included a letter that outlined her life and service in Calcutta.

Weeks and then months went by with no response from Rome. Finally in July 1948, Archbishop Périer summoned Father Van Exem to his office. He had received news from the Vatican that very afternoon. Rome had granted Mother Teresa's request for exclaustration. She would be allowed to remain a member of the Loreto Order and work outside of the convent. It was a wonderful victory for Mother Teresa and a vindication of the very principals that the Loreto Sisters' founder, Mary Ward, had been denied. There was, however, one condition: Mother Teresa would remain outside the cloister for a year, at which time, the archbishop would review her progress and decide whether she would return to the convent.

The archbishop also made it clear to Father Van Exem that the news from Rome was not to be given to Mother Teresa until after the school week was completed. Despite Mother Teresa's appeals to be told of the decision, the archbishop was adamant: she would be told the following Sunday. An elated Father Van Exem agreed to the archbishop's request.

On Sunday, August 8, 1948, Father Van Exem arose as usual and celebrated mass in the chapel at the Loreto convent. Following his usual custom, he gave the first sermon in Bengali, and then, after mass was concluded, another sermon in Hindi. He then asked Mother Teresa to meet with him in the convent parlor. When she arrived, he told her that he had received news from Rome. According to his account, Mother Teresa turned pale and requested to go to the chapel to pray. When she returned, he gave her the good news: not only did Rome agree to her request to leave the convent, but also that she continue her life as a Loreto Sister. She then signed three copies of the permission: one for Rome, one for the archbishop, and one for herself. She then asked, "Can I go to the slums now?"[6]

## AN EMOTIONAL DEPARTURE

Despite Mother Teresa's willingness to leave immediately to begin her work, there was still much to be done to prepare for her departure. First, she needed to inform the convent that she was leaving. Archbishop Périer had feared a shocked reaction from the sisters. His fears were justified. When the decree was made public, the mother superior took to her bed for a week. Another sister wept uncontrollably; many were shocked at the announcement or mystified as to why one of their own, particularly one who seemed happy in her surroundings, would want to leave the convent. Those close to Mother Teresa worried about her health and whether she could sustain a rigorous life on the Calcutta streets. A notice posted on a Loreto blackboard requested that the sisters not criticize or praise Mother Teresa, but pray for her and her decision.

In preparation for her departure from the convent, Mother Teresa purchased three saris from a local bazaar. Each one was white with three blue stripes; this simple garment would become the distinctive habit of her new order. The fabric was the cheapest available at the time, and was of the kind usually worn by poor Bengali women. The blue stripes held a special meaning for Mother Teresa, as the color is usually associated with the Virgin Mary. Father Van Exem later blessed the garments, along with a small cross and rosary, which had been placed on each garment in the St. Mary's chapel while Father Henry and another nun watched. Among the last tasks that needed to be done required Father Van Exem's help. Mother Teresa needed to write a letter to her mother, explaining all that had happened. She believed that if her spiritual advisor also wrote the letter, that would settle any fears or worries her mother might have about her daughter's decision to leave Loreto.

Father Van Exem suggested that Mother Teresa take some medical training. Working in the slums, there would be plenty of opportunity to offer medical assistance. She agreed and decided to go to Patna in the state of Bihar where she would receive training from the Medical Mission Sisters at their hospital. Archbishop Périer supported the decision and Sister Stephanie Ingendaa, the mother superior at the hospital, warmly agreed to the request to help Mother Teresa in whatever way the sisters could.

On August 16, a week after learning of the Vatican's decision, Mother Teresa changed her clothes. The long black habit, with its floor-length skirt, the white coif, and black veil were laid aside. She now wore her new religious habit, a symbolic breaking with the religious uniform she had worn for the past two decades. Even though many of her former pupils wished to see their teacher in a sari, her leaving was a solitary affair. That evening, she left the convent grounds in a taxi as quietly as she had come almost 20 years before. In her pocket, she carried five rupees and a ticket to Patna.

## A NEW BEGINNING

On August 17, Mother Teresa arrived at Patna, an old city located on the banks of the Ganges River. Sister Stephanie was there waiting to welcome her. They went together to the Holy Family Hospital, where Mother Teresa would spend the next few months receiving her medical training.

The hospital and convent buildings were located in the poorer section of Patna, known as Padri ki Haveli (House of the Fathers), and was named after the first church built in the town. The Holy Family Hospital, which formerly served as a school building, was modest: two stories high with a small separate building to one side that housed the operating and delivery rooms. The hospital was staffed by nuns who were doctors, mainly gynecologists, obstetricians, and surgeons. Other nuns served as nurses, laboratory technicians, and nutritionists. The hospital also housed a nursing school that many Indian girls attended.

The convent where Mother Teresa would take her meals and sleep occupied part of the former church. Built of stone blocks, it had a high ceiling, a worn stone floor, small gothic-shaped windows, and whitewashed walls. The main part of the church was divided into small cubicles by bamboo rods and white cotton sheets. The garden was once the cemetery; on very hot nights, many slept between the tombstones covered with mosquito netting. The hopsital staff ate in the former servant's quarters with an old Hindu cook maintaining the small kitchen.

Because the hospital was so busy, there was little fanfare to welcome Mother Teresa. Instead, she was put into a cubicle, given a chair in the dining room, and included in the day-to-day running of the hospital. Many of the sisters realized that she was in a period of transition, and while Mother Teresa knew what she was to do, she was still unclear about how she was to carry out her calling. In the meantime, the Medical Mission Sisters tried to make her feel at home and helped prepare her for the grueling work ahead.

Now, instead of lecturing students, Mother Teresa's days were filled with new experiences; she never knew what to expect from one day to the next. Whenever there was a new admission, an impending birth-or-operation, Mother Teresa was summoned at the same time as a doctor was called. This experience not only gave Mother Teresa an opportunity to practice her Hindi, in which she was not very fluent, but to become acquainted with expectant mothers, fatal accidents, ill and abandoned children, and death on the operating table.

She also learned to tend to patients ill and dying with cholera or smallpox. One nun remembered that, no matter what the calamity, Mother Teresa remained unfazed by it, maintaining her focus on the patient. She could always be counted on to hold a dying patient's hand, to comfort a small child frightened by the hospital, or to cradle a newborn infant in her arms. She learned how to do many simple medical procedures such as making a hospital bed, giving injections, and administering medicines. She helped assist in delivering babies, something in which she took special delight. Working with the nutritionists, Mother Teresa learned about the importance of a healthy diet, hygiene, and adequate rest. This knowledge was key to carrying out her work in the slums. As Mother Teresa came to know many of the poor families of the area, she attended weddings, feasts, and funerals, slowly entering their world and becoming one of them.

During her time at Patna, Mother Teresa gained her first associate. A young girl, suffering from advanced stages of tuberculosis, asked Mother Teresa whether she could help her in serving the poor. Toward the end of her stay at Holy Family, she appointed the young girl as an associate in her work. Her new helper ministered to other patients sick with tuberculosis and offered prayers for the recovery of those stricken with the disease. Unfortunately, she did not accompany Mother Teresa to Calcutta for she died at Holy Family soon after.

## BUILDING A FOUNDATION

During the evenings when not working at the hospital, Mother Teresa discussed her plans with the many members of the Medical Mission Sisters. She welcomed ideas, practical suggestions, and criticism from the others about how she should best implement her plans. One thing that did become clear: if Mother Teresa's proposed order wanted to work with the poor, they would have to commit themselves to working *only* for the poor.

Out of these discussions came the foundation for Mother Teresa's congregation as well as many of the rules and routines that the group would follow. Perhaps the most valuable lesson was the rule of balance as practiced by the founding mother of the Medical Mission Sisters, Mother Anna Dengel. Like Mother Teresa, Dengal also had to obtain special permission from the Vatican in order to establish an order of nuns who were also practicing surgeons and midwives. Among Mother Dengel's tenets was that heavy tasks, physical or emotional, could not be carried out for long without rest and renewal. Therefore, it was imperative for her nuns to take regular rests when needed and retreats to recharge their bodies and minds.

The sisters suggested that with the poor living conditions and hard work that was to be done everyday, prayer should be strictly observed, but no prayer should be scheduled after 9 P.M. This would allow the nuns plenty of rest and relaxation. There should be plenty of protein-rich food for meals, especially at breakfast, but the selection should be simple; no exceptions to meals were to be made except in cases of illness. Mother Teresa had thought that she and her nuns would eat nothing more than rice and salt, the basic diet of the poor. But she learned that this diet was too sparse; she and her nuns would then be unable to work efficiently at their jobs. This kind of diet also left one open to the very diseases of the poor that Mother Teresa hoped to treat and fight. Mother Teresa sagely took the advice given to her.

Mother Teresa envisioned an eight-hour workday beginning at five in the morning. For that schedule to work, the Medical Missionaries suggested there be one daily hour of rest so that the nuns would have the energy to carry out their tasks. They also suggested that one day a week should be taken off, usually a Sunday, but for those who worked Sundays, one full day of rest should be scheduled sometime during the week. There should also be an annual retreat for all, which took place away from their work. Clothing should remain simple; the Medical Mission Sisters wore white cotton habits and veils that were changed everyday, sometimes even twice a day. When Mother Teresa explained that the white cotton sari was to be the habit, the nuns suggested that for the sake of health, all saris should be washed everyday, and each nun should be given three saris: one to wear, one to wash, and one for special occasions and emergencies. Head coverings, while necessary to protect oneself from the hot Indian summers, were to be kept to a minimum with no starch used on any part of the headdress veil.

## TIME TO LEAVE

After only a few weeks, Mother Teresa wrote to Father Van Exem asking for permission to go to Calcutta. She felt she had learned all that she could for now, and was anxious to begin her work. Reading her request, Father Van Exem was skeptical. Mother Teresa had been with the Medical Mission Sisters for too short a time. He had fully expected her to stay much longer: at least six months, even up to a year. The archbishop felt similarly; both men wanted Mother Teresa to stay longer, to make sure she had taken advantage of every opportunity for her medical training.

Still, her letters kept coming, asking for permission to leave for Calcutta. She had learned all she could, plus receiving knowledge about diseases that she most likely would not encounter in the city's slums. Further, she argued, she would learn more about cholera, sores, and other diseases that were prevalent in the slums if she were living and working among the poor who suffered from them. The Medical Missionaries agreed with Mother Teresa; it was time for Mother Teresa to begin her mission.

Not convinced, Father Van Exem traveled to Patna to meet with Mother Teresa and Sister Stephanie to discuss what was to be done. When he arrived at Holy Family, he looked for Mother Teresa, but could not find her in the group of nurses at the hospital. Finally, a small voice answered, "But Father, I am here."[7] Father Van Exem, having never seen Mother Teresa in her sari, completely overlooked her.

Meeting with Sister Stephanie and the sister-doctor who had been overseeing Mother Teresa, Father Van Exem listened as the two explained why it was time for Mother Teresa to leave. She was ready to begin her life in the slums they told him, and they would always be there should she need advice or direction in medical matters. Father Van Exem then explained that both he and the archbishop were concerned about the possibility of a church scandal should Mother Teresa fail in her mission. She would not make a mistake, the sisters assured him, and again they reminded him that there were others who would share in the responsibility of her undertaking. Finding himself outnumbered, Father Van Exem relented: Mother Teresa could go to Calcutta.

## NOTES

1. Navin Chawla, *Mother Teresa: The Authorized Biography* (Rockport, Mass.: Element, 1992), p. 21.

2. Kathryn Spink, *Mother Teresa* (San Francisco: Harper & Row, 1997), p. 24.

3. Edward Le Joly, *Mother Teresa of Calcutta: A Biography* (San Francisco: Harper & Row, 1977), pp. 10–11.

4. Le Joly, *Mother Teresa*, p. 12.

5. Spink, *Mother Teresa*, p. 29.

6. Eileen Egan, *Such a Vision of the Street: Mother Teresa—The Spirit and the Work* (Garden City, N.Y.: Image Books, 1986), p. 35.

7. Spink, *Mother Teresa*, p. 33.

# Chapter 4

# OUT OF A CESSPOOL—HOPE

Shortly after his visit with Mother Teresa and the Medical Mission Sisters, Father Van Exem wrote to Mother Teresa that the archbishop had relented and given his permission for her to return to Calcutta. He had also found a place for her to live with the Little Sisters of the Poor. She arrived at the St. Joseph's Home for the elderly, located at 2 Lower Circular Road, on December 9, 1948. It had been barely four months since she had left the Loreto convent in Entally and started her training in Patna. Prior to her leaving Patna, Mother Teresa spoke with one of the nun-doctors in the cemetery of the convent grounds. Remarking that she had no idea how she was going to proceed or where she would even begin, Mother Teresa nonetheless remained confident that God would direct her. And with that thought, she made her way back to Calcutta to undertake her life's work.

Although Calcutta had the third highest per-capita income in India, it was a vast sea of suffering and despair. The streets, where people were born and died hourly, were crowded with beggars and lepers, together with a host of refugees from the countryside who had never known a home. Unwanted infants were regularly abandoned and left to die in clinics, on the streets, or in garbage bins. There were thousands of pavement dwellers within the city itself; 44 percent of the city did not have sewers. It was into this sea of misery that Mother Teresa now came.

The St. Joseph's Home proved to be a good choice for Mother Teresa. The Little Sisters of the Poor lived in strict poverty. Although they worked through other institutions, they had no regular source of income to draw on and were completely dependent on donations of food and money. This dependence on God and the charity of others became an important element with the Missionaries of Charity as well. Although the mother superior was at first unsure about whether Mother Teresa could stay at the St. Joseph's Home, Father Van Exem assured her that Mother Teresa had received a decree of exclaustration and that she was still answerable to the archbishop.

Upon her arrival, Mother Teresa made a short retreat under Father Van Exem's guidance. They decided to meet every morning; she would spend afternoons in prayer and meditation. She also spent part of her time during those first days at the convent helping the sisters care for their aged patients.

## MOTIJIHL

On December 21, 1948, Mother Teresa left her small room on the first floor near the gate of St. Joseph's and went to mass. After breakfast, she left the convent grounds and boarded a bus bound for Mauli Ali to begin her work. She was dressed in her white sari, but she wore it not as a poor Bengali woman but instead wrapped around her head covering a tiny cotton cap. Completing her habit was a small black crucifix, attached to her left shoulder by a safety pin. Under her rough leather sandals, a gift from the Patna sisters, she wore no stockings. With a meager lunch in a small packet she entered the world of the Calcutta slums.

Her first stop was in the slum of Motijihl, which means "Pearl Lake." While there was no lake, there was a large brackish sump in the center of the neighborhood that provided the area's residents with water. Raw sewage flowed into open drains and garbage lay piled on the streets. The slum's residents lived in small hovels with dirt floors. There was no school, no hospital, and no dispensary.

Motijihl was already a familiar place for Mother Teresa. Though she had never personally visited it, many sodality students at St. Mary's, under Father Henry's direction, had come to work in the area. Father Henry was more than eager to offer help to Mother Teresa and provided her with a list of families whose children had attended the school at the Loreto convent. Mother Teresa visited with as many families as she could. She told them she had permission to start a school right in the area. As a result, several parents promised to send their children to her the next morning.

## BEGINNING RIGHT ON THE GROUND

The next morning, Mother Teresa was back in Motijihl and was happy to see several children waiting for her on the steps of a railway bridge that led down into the slum. In trying to find a spot where they could meet, Mother Teresa noticed that the only open area was a tree near the sump. With no blackboard, chalk, books, or desks, Mother Teresa took a stick and used it to write in the mud. As the children squatted and watched, she traced the letters of the Bengali alphabet with the stick. Mother Teresa had made a start, or as she would later describe it, beginning "right on the ground,"[1] which became one of the defining concepts of the constitution of the Missionaries of Charity.

Soon the number of pupils attending classes multiplied as word spread that a school had been started in Motijihl. In time, the sounds of children reciting the alphabet competed with the other everyday noises of the slum. When morning lessons were finished, Mother Teresa looked for someplace to eat her small lunch, seeking out a quiet spot where she could find drinking water. Once, when she stopped at a local convent to ask if she could come inside to take her meal, the nuns, thinking Mother Teresa was a beggar, refused. Instead, they directed her to the back to eat under the stairs where the other beggars ate. In later years, she would never mention the name of the convent that had turned her away.

Mother Teresa became a familiar, if strange, sight on the Calcutta streets: many watched as the lone woman, dressed like a poor Indian, spent her time visiting in the alleyways and mean streets of the slums. Even one of her strongest supporters, Father Michael Gabric, a Jesuit priest from Yugoslavia and a member of the missionary group whose actions first influenced Mother Teresa as a young girl, was puzzled by her actions. He candidly admitted in an interview, "We thought she was cracked."[2]

At the request of the archbishop, Mother Teresa kept a record of her early efforts, dating from December 25, 1948 until June 11, 1949. Only a small part of this fascinating record survives. These pages are her accounts of her first days working in Motijihl, especially with the children. Children who were dirty were given a bath. After lessons in hygiene and reading, she helped the children learn their catechism. She noted especially the joy the children gave her, remembering how she laughed when teaching them.

There were also entries in which Mother Teresa described moments when humor was of a darker nature. Attending to one poor man who had a gangrenous thumb, Mother Teresa realized that the thumb would have to be amputated. Saying a prayer and taking a pair of scissors, she snipped it off. Her patient then fainted in one direction and she in the other. She often gave her bus fare away to those who needed it more and, instead, walked home.

## THE DARK NIGHT

Although the remaining pages of her journal document the people and situations that she saw and even the feelings she had while doing her work, it is still hard to imagine the tremendous loneliness that Mother Teresa must have felt as she made her way through the slums of Calcutta in those first months. For someone who had been accustomed to the order and peace of convent life, the reality must have been jarring. But Mother Teresa's faith in God was absolute, and so she kept up her work, despite the exhaustion and pain she felt at the end of the day.

Her faith also kept Mother Teresa from falling into despair, for she sensed that her work accomplished very little. Calcutta faced intractable problems. Since winning independence from Great Britain, India had been divided into two nations: Muslim Pakistan and Hindu India. Despite the creation of a separate country for Muslims, conflict between them and the Hindus continued, sometimes erupting into bloody violence, which left families devastated and areas ravaged. Many Hindus seeking jobs flooded the streets of an already-overcrowded Calcutta. Most ended up in the streets, and with a growing shortage of food and water, many were plunged into unrelenting poverty. Much of the food and water available became contaminated from the overflowing sewage. Many considered the acquisition of one rupee (about 11 cents American) as good fortune.

Still, Mother Teresa persevered. As people heard of what she was doing, they came forth with money, supplies, time, and favors. The bus driver who drove the route to St. Joseph's made her sit in a seat next to him so she should would not have to make the hour-long walk back to St. Joseph's. A former teacher at St. Mary's came to help her teach classes. On one occasion, she went to a local parish priest for help. As much as he said he was glad to be of service, he offered her little in the way of encouragement or help. Mother Teresa then went to another priest who was so delighted with what she had accomplished, that he presented her with a gift of 100 rupees to help carry on her work. It was a princely sum that allowed Mother Teresa to rent two small huts in Motijihl for five rupees each. One hut served as a school where the students met for class and where they were given milk at lunchtime and free bars of soap as prizes.

The infectious enthusiasm of the children spread throughout the munity. Here and there, people came forward with small gifts fo. school: a stool, an odd table, even books and slates appeared. By Jani 4, 1949, less than two weeks after she first set out, Mother Teresa haa a schoolhouse, over 50 students, and three teachers to help her. Not only were the children learning their alphabet and numbers, but classes in needlework were offered for the young girls as well as the continuing emphasis on teaching the children hygiene and catechism. The school was soon formally blessed. It was one of Mother Teresa's greatest successes.

The other hut on the premises was used for a more solemn purpose: caring for the ill and dying poor, a place where Mother Teresa offered comfort, solace, and, above all, dignity to those who had no home and no hope. Her reasons for creating the small hostel arose out of one of her many experiences in dealing with the poorest of the poor. One day, Mother Teresa saw a woman dying on the street beside a hospital. She picked the woman up and took her to the hospital but was refused admission because the woman had no money. The woman later died on the street. Mother Teresa then realized that she must make a home for the dying.

Still, she was plagued by doubt about whether she was doing the work God had called her to do. There were moments when she wished to return to the quiet and security that the Loreto convent offered. On one occasion when she approached a priest for financial aid, he treated her as if she were doing something wrong by begging, telling her to ask instead her own parish priest for money. He left her saying he did not understand and brusquely turned away. The experience reduced Mother Teresa to tears and raised grave self-doubts. She would later say that God was training her; but in order to carry out His will, she had to feel completely useless and inadequate to the task before her. Continually, she struggled to turn her will aside and place her faith completely with God in the hope that He would continue to show her the way. She later wrote of this period as the "dark night of the birth"[3] of her order, the Missionaries of Charity.

But in her begging for food, medicine, clothing, and money, Mother Teresa was actually carrying out a time-honored tradition of mendicancy. Throughout much of India's history, priests, holy men, and teachers depended on the support of the community for their livelihood. Her begging letters and begging expeditions were a natural outgrowth of her own poverty and a dependence on providence to provide for her basic needs and the needs of those she helped. Although in some western cultures such overt dependence is often looked down upon, in India, as well as in traditional Roman Catholic practice, begging was nothing to be ashamed about.

## 14 CREEK LANE

During her first months on the Calcutta streets, Mother Teresa's spiritual advisor, Father Van Exem, watched carefully to see how she was holding up. After talking, both he and she decided that it was time for her to have a place of her own where she could start her work and no longer impose on the Little Sisters of the Poor. But Mother Teresa's first efforts to find affordable housing met with little success. Often landlords would not keep their appointments. Others, upon seeing the strange European nun with no visible means of support, refused outright to rent to her. Mother Teresa did not lose heart, but identified her plight with that of the people she served. She later wrote:

> Our Lord just wants me to be a "Free Nun," covered with the poverty of the Cross. But today I have learned a good lesson— the poverty of the poor must often be too hard for them.... I walked and walked till my legs and arms ached. I thought how they must also ache in body and soul, looking for home, food, help."[4]

Father Van Exem finally stepped in. He spoke to a member of a Bengali Catholic family, Albert Gomes, who, along with his brothers, owned a sizeable property at 14 Creek Lane in East Calcutta. One brother, Michael Gomes, lived in the house with his family. Finally an agreement was reached in which Mother Teresa would move into a room on the second floor. She would pay no rent. The home's location was later described by Mother Teresa as "rich in its poverty."[5]

In February 1949, she moved into her new quarters, bringing with her only a small suitcase. Her room was spartan in appearance: a single chair, a packing case for a desk, and some extra wooden boxes for seats. The wall was adorned with an image of the Virgin Mary, a gift from Father Van Exem who had originally received it from Mother Teresa as a Christmas gift years before.

Mother Teresa now had some helpers who accompanied her so that she would not be alone in the slums. Charur Ma, a widow who was the cook at St. Mary's at Entally, often went with her on shopping trips. Mable Gomes, the young daughter of the family with whom she boarded, also went with Mother Teresa on occasion. Even Michael Gomes, when he had time, went with Mother Teresa to chemists' shops, similar to American pharmacies, to ask for donations of medical supplies. Father Van Exem sent a parish worker to accompany her on some of her daily visits to the poor and dying. She was even joined by some of her former students who came to visit her. Seeing her in her sari, some burst into tears. But all were glad to see her and to offer what help they could.

Many years later, Michael Gomes recounted some of his experiences helping Mother Teresa. On one rainy afternoon, Mother Teresa and Mable Gomes returned from the slums. Both were soaking wet, and Mother Teresa apologized for Mable's condition. She told Michael that they had just come from a home where they found a woman standing in a room without a roof. Knee-deep in water, the woman had held an enamel washbasin over the head of her sick child to protect him from the rain. The landlord had broken the roof deliberately because the woman had been unable to pay her rent for the last two months, owing him a total of eight rupees. Later that afternoon, Mother Teresa hurried back to give the woman her rent money.

On another occasion, when Michael accompanied Mother Teresa on one of her begging forays, they again encountered rainy weather. Watching from the train window, they saw a man, completely drenched, slumped under a tree. The two hurried to finish collecting medicines and went back with the hopes of helping the man. However, when they reached him, he was already dead. As Gomes later recounted, Mother Teresa was in anguish over the incident, and the fact that many other poor and gravely ill men and women, like the unknown man, might have wanted to say something to someone, to have some comfort in their final hours. The incident hardened her resolve to search for a facility where the terminally ill could die in dignity and peace.

Gomes also remembered giving Mother Teresa extra food whenever there was any to spare. Often she would ask him for extra mugs of rice, which she gave away to starving families. Still, from time to time, she encountered hostility. Gomes remembered when a group of passengers on a train, remarking on her strange nun's habit, said that she was nothing more than a Christian hoping to convert Hindus. For a long time, Mother Teresa listened in silence. Finally she turned to them and said, "Ami Bharater Bharat Amar" (I am Indian and India is mine).[6] The passenger car was silent for the rest of the trip.

## "IT WILL BE A HARD LIFE"

On March 19, 1949, the feast day of St. Joseph, foster father of Jesus and the protector of the Virgin Mary, a young girl appeared at 14 Creek Lane. Subashni Das had been a boarder at St. Mary's at Entally since she was a small girl, and had been one of Mother Teresa's students. She was now in the last year of secondary school. She had come to join Mother

Teresa in her work. Mother Teresa remarked, "It will be a hard life. Are you prepared for it?"[7] The young woman said yes, and in doing so became Mother Teresa's first postulant, taking the name of Agnes, Mother Teresa's Christian name. She would, in time, become Mother Teresa's closest aide: she replaced Mother Teresa as the mistress of novices, the nun who oversees the training of new nuns, and took over the duties of the mother superior when Mother Teresa began traveling.

Some weeks later, another former student Magdalena Gomes also came to the house. She, too, wished to join Mother Teresa in helping the poor. She took the name of Sister Gertrude and became the order's first doctor. By Easter of that year, the three women were sharing the tiny quarters at the Gomes's home and traveling everyday to Motijihl. They lived as nuns, though the Church had not yet recognized them as a formal religious order.

Soon, two more women arrived to join them. By the beginning of summer, there were 10 young women, all former students of Mother Teresa, living at the Gomes's home. Since none had graduated from school, Mother Teresa made sure that they completed their studies and that they all passed their final exams. Of the original 10, only 2 eventually left. The others went on to become some of the first novitiates of Mother Teresa's Missionaries of Charity.

To make room for the new arrivals, the Gomes's opened the upper room, which was really more like a large loft. The group used one area of the room as a chapel. Father Henry donated a wood altar and candlesticks. Above the altar was the picture of the Virgin Mother that Father Van Exem had given to Mother Teresa.

Mother Teresa instituted a schedule for the young women. Each morning, they were awakened by a bell, which also summoned them to meals. The same bell also signaled periods of prayer, rest, and work. Every morning, clad in their saris, the young women and Mother Teresa left for the poorest areas of Calcutta. The days followed a set routine: mornings were spent teaching school, while afternoons were given to the sick and dying. By this time, there were two schools to tend to: the first one in Motijihl and another in the slum of Tiljala, where Mother Teresa rented another small room for her new students.

The young women and Mother Teresa also established a dispensary, which was located in a classroom in the local parish school. After school hours, the large room was turned into a screening room for tuberculosis patients. The classroom, which opened onto a veranda, was often the scene of long lines of people waiting to be examined. The nuns tried to get the most seriously ill into city hospitals. However, when necessary, they cared for the sick on the spot as they lay in the streets and alleys of the city.

Mother Teresa worried about her charges. Remembering the advice of the sisters at Patna, she was especially concerned that they were getting enough to eat. Michael Gomes remembers one instance in which Mother Teresa, sitting in the back of a truck with some bags of rice and flour, returned at the end of the day from one of her begging expeditions. She had not eaten all day nor gotten any water for fear that someone would steal the food meant for her postulants. She went without in order that the food would be delivered safely to the house.

To help the sisters, Father Van Exem and Father Henry made an announcement at Sunday mass calling for *mushti bhikka*, a Bengali custom where any families that were able put aside a handful of rice for a beggar. This effort marked the start of the feeding program that the Missionaries of Charity oversaw and that would in time include not only food, but clothing and soap for the poor.

## A YEAR'S END

And then the first year was over. On August 16, 1949, Mother Teresa's year of exclaustration came to an end. Now Archbishop Périer had to decide whether she would remain outside the cloister of Loreto or return. By this time, the archbishop had received reports of Mother Teresa and her growing band of young women. In his mind, there was no turning back for Mother Teresa; she would remain outside of the cloister. If she had returned, the young women would have disbanded. They were not recognized as a formal order of nuns; they were simply a group of very religious women who happened to be living with a rather unorthodox nun. A course that would allow Mother Teresa to continue her work with her assistants would be to accept them as a congregation for the diocese of Calcutta answerable to the archbishop just as Mother Teresa was. This was a real possibility since the little group now numbered more than 10, the required number needed to begin a new congregation.

Still, the archbishop remained cautious. Before making any decision, he needed to know if there had been any negative reports about Mother Teresa and her work. He went to Father Van Exem, who admitted that there had been one report, that of an old Jesuit who believed Mother Teresa was doing the work of the devil. He had gone to the mother superior at Loreto, asking her why a woman who was doing such a fine job as a teacher in an established school would leave to wander about the slums of Calcutta. The archbishop, so incensed by the comments, insisted that the

priest in question immediately apologize to the superior for his criticism of
Mother Teresa and her work.

While Mother Teresa awaited the archbishop's decision, she took another very important step: she applied for and was granted Indian citizen-
ship. The act was a potent one, signifying not only her break with her
European roots, but a pledge to become one with the people she served.
By the end of 1949, the archbishop had become so supportive of Mother
Teresa and her efforts that he stated his willingness to recognize her group
as a congregation in his archdiocese. The final approval would have to
come from Rome, but the archbishop was willing to make the journey
himself and plead Mother Teresa's case on her behalf. He planned to go to
Rome in April 1950 to present the Vatican with the necessary documents.

Now Mother Teresa struggled with a draft of the proposed order's constitution, which outlined the rules by which the nuns would live. She
wrote of her spiritual calling on the train ride to Darjeeling and outlined
the first three vows all would take when coming into the order: poverty,
chastity, and obedience. To these she added a fourth vow: "to give whole-
hearted and free service to the poorest of the poor,"[8] which would become
known as "our way."[9] She also decided on a name for the new order: the
Missionaries of Charity.

She turned over her draft to Father Van Exem, who worked on it, tight-
ening up the language, as Mother Teresa's grasp of English was not good.
Father Van Exem forwarded the document to a priest who specialized in
canon, or church, law. Then five copies were made and taken to the archbishop who presented the documents to Cardinal Pietro Fumosoni-
Biondi, head of the Office for the Propagation of the Faith for the
Catholic Church. The Vatican accepted the constitution, even with the
fourth vow, which over time brought many to the order and quieted even
the most skeptical. On October 7, 1950, the church had a new congregation in its fold: the Missionaries of Charity, headed by Mother Teresa.

## DRAWING ON THE PAST FOR THE FUTURE

The new constitution of the Missionaries of Charity may have been
polished by the priests of the church, but the document reflected the spirit
of Mother Teresa. In it, she not only outlined why she believed what she
was doing was so important and the specific vows for her new order, but
also some basic rules that the Missionaries of Charity continue to follow
today. She began by stating the goal of the order:

> Our aim is to quench the infinite thirst of Jesus Christ for love
> by the profession of the evangelical counsels and by whole-

hearted free service to the poorest of the poor, according to the teaching and the life of our Lord in the gospel, revealing in a unique way the salvation of God.... Our particular mission is to labor at the salvation and sanctification of the poorest of the poor.... We are called THE MISSIONARIES OF CHARITY.[10]

Mother Teresa wished to see the vow of poverty rigorously applied. She wrote:

Whoever the poorest of the poor are, they are Christ for us—Christ under the guise of humans suffering....Our food, our dress; it must be just like the poor. The poor are Christ himself. We should not serve the poor like they *were* Jesus. We should serve the poor because they *are* Jesus.[11]

Mother Teresa sought to reinforce the vow of poverty in other ways, too. In the constitution of the order it is stipulated that at no time will the Missionaries of Charity own any buildings or other property. Postulants were to be members of the Roman Catholic Church, which would preserve the very core of the congregation. However, in time it became clear that because the church was not a strong institution in India, that this stipulation would have to be modified. Still, the core tenets of the constitution for the new congregation showed the influence of those groups that had the greatest impact on Mother Teresa's own life, from the missionary efforts of the Jesuits who swore devotion to the Sacred Heart of Jesus and obedience to God, and also to the Loreto Sisters who stressed a similar devotion and obedience to carrying out the work of the Lord on earth.

The last matter that needed to be attended to was the question of the sisters' dress. Sent to Rome were three photographs: one depicting a postulant in a plain white sari and short-sleeved habit, the second of a novice in a white sari and habit with sleeves that entirely covered the arm, and last a picture of Mother Teresa in the sisters' dress of white sari with the distinctive blue border. The new style of dress, while unorthodox, was accepted.

## A NEW BEGINNING

On October 7, 1950, Archbishop Périer came to the house at 14 Creek Lane for the first time to celebrate mass at the altar located in the tiny chapel on the second floor. A large number of persons assembled to hear Father Van Exem read the decree of erection recognizing the Missionaries of Charity as a new congregation limited to the diocese of Calcutta. That same day, 11 young women began their lives as postulates of the new order. It was a joyous occasion for all.

Over the next two years, 29 young women joined Mother Teresa. All took up residency on the second floor of the Gomes's house, which resonated with their activity. Mother Teresa wrote in her journal of the trust, surrender, and cheerfulness of the newcomers. She observed with special pride how dutifully they accepted the vow of poverty required of them.

It was not an easy life. The novices washed their clothes and their bodies using communal buckets. They cleaned their teeth with ashes and slept on thin pallets. Their meager pile of garments consisted only of their cotton saris, coarse underwear, a pair of sandals, a crucifix pinned to the left shoulder, a rosary, and an umbrella to protect them from the monsoon rains. All these items were packed in a small bundle (*potla*), which they used as a pillow.

To celebrate the completion of the new nun's postulancy, or taking of vows, Father Van Exem created a special ceremony. The novices came to the cathedral dressed as Bengali brides. During the service, they went to a room where Mother Teresa cut their hair. This practice represented a tremendous sacrifice, as many Bengali girls regarded their long hair as a great gift. The women's hair was often so long that the entire process took several hours to complete. They then reappeared in their religious habits as novices. It was a beautiful ceremony and one that Mother Teresa completely approved for its incorporation of high church ritual with the local culture. Father Van Exem remembered with some amusement the reaction of the locals to the first ceremonies of this kind: "The ordination of a priest takes two hours, the consecration of a bishop three hours, the reception of a Missionary of Charity four hours!"[12] Not everyone, however, was pleased at the spectacle of young Bengal brides who were in fact not really married but had entered into the Catholic Church.

It was soon apparent that the quarters at Creek Lane were becoming too small for the growing number of sisters. Father Van Exem and Father Henry once again went to work searching for new quarters for the order. One of the first nuns to join the order remembered how Mother Teresa and her nuns helped the two priests:

> Father Henry organized a procession every evening. He accompanied the sisters as we went through the Calcutta streets saying the rosary aloud.... And from six to nine, we went on the road from our house to St. Teresa's Church and hence to Fatima Chapel, praying there and again on our way home. We

were asking our Lady of Fatima to obtain for us the new house we needed.[13]

Finally, a suitable house was found at 54A Lower Circular Road. The home, which belonged to a former Muslim magistrate, was bought by the diocese of Calcutta with the understanding that Mother Teresa would pay back the loan. In February 1953, Mother Teresa and her group moved into their new residence. In tribute to their founder, the sisters called it Motherhouse.

## NOTES

1. Eileen Egan, *Such a Vision of the Street: Mother Teresa—The Spirit and the Work* (Garden City, N.Y.: Image Books, 1986), p. 43.

2. Egan, *Vision*, p. 43.

3. Raghu Rai and Navin Chawla, *Faith and Compassion: The Life and Work of Mother Teresa*, (Rockport, Mass.: Element, 1999), p. 39.

4. Rai and Chawla, *Faith*, p. 38.

5. Kathryn Spink, *Mother Teresa: A Complete Authorized Biography* (San Francisco: Harper & Row, 1997), p. 38.

6. Rai and Chawla, *Faith*, p. 40.

7. Rai and Chawla, *Faith*, p. 40.

8. Egan, *Vision*, p. 48.

9. Rai and Chawla, *Faith*, p. 42.

10. Edward Le Joly, *Mother Teresa of Calcutta: A Biography* (San Francisco: Harper & Row, 1977), p. 28.

11. Mother Teresa with Jose Luis Gonzàles-Balado, *Mother Teresa: In My Own Words* (New York: Gramercy Books, 1996), pp. 24, 30.

12. Spink, *Mother Teresa*, p. 43.

13. Le Joly, *Mother Teresa*, p. 30.

# Chapter 5

# "RIGOROUS POVERTY IS OUR SAFEGUARD"

Lower Circular Road is a humming center of activity in Calcutta. The street is filled with pedestrians and traffic. The everyday drone of people, car horns, rickshaw bells, and trams is broken occasionally by the passing of Hindu processions and political parades. With all the commotion, it is easy to overlook the residence located at 54A Lower Circular Road; the noise of the everyday world drowns out the daily prayers of the home's residents.

To get to 54A Lower Circular Road, one takes a narrow lane that leads to a three-storied, gray-washed building. On closer inspection, however, one sees that there are really two houses that surround a small courtyard. Leaving the lane takes one to the front brown-painted door; here is a small chain attached to the frame, which, when pulled, rings a bell on the inside. The bell is an acknowledgement of the power outages that often plague Calcutta. Once inside the home, the visitor is in a very special place: the center of activity for the Missionaries of Charity and their now-deceased founder, Mother Teresa.

## POOR BY CHOICE

With their move into Motherhouse in early 1953, the Missionaries of Charity had their own base of operations. Not only did the new residence offer more room for the growing number of newcomers to the order; it also had its own chapel and a dining hall. Mother Teresa also had her own quarters. Slowly, new recruits appeared asking to be taken into the congregation as a Missionary of Charity.

e the spacious new surroundings, Mother Teresa was determined
congregation live a life shaped by extreme poverty. They would
deny themselves the necessities; however, they would reject with
kind, but firm, graciousness any offers of material goods from the well in-
tentioned, as they were seen by the order as luxuries. "Our rigorous
poverty is our safeguard," Mother Teresa said. She later explained that the
Missionaries of Charity did not want to do what other religious orders had
done throughout history—that is, to begin by serving the poor, but end-
ing up servicing the rich, and themselves. "In order to understand and
help those who have nothing, we must live like them.... The only difference is that they are poor by birth and we are poor by choice."[1]

In the early days of the order, maintaining the vows of poverty was not
that difficult. Besides their meager possessions, the sisters soon learned
how to beg for their needs as well as the needs of the poor. However, the
poor came first and the needs of the order second. Still, that period was
filled with a number of stories, many of them humorous, as the sisters
learned to improvise given their situation and their mission.

Finding properly fitting shoes was a continual challenge for the nuns.
On one occasion, Mother Teresa allocated the same pair of sandals to
three different sisters, all of whom were in desperate need of footwear. On
another occasion, the only pair of shoes available for one sister to wear to
church services was a pair of red stiletto heels. However, she chose to wear
them and the sight of her hobbling was the source of much amusement for
many days.

Articles of clothing were also at a premium; habits were made out of
old bulgur wheat sacks; sometimes the labels were still visible under the
thin cloth cover of the white saris, even after repeated washings. One sister's habit clearly bore the label Not for Resale under her sari. One Christmas, there were not enough shawls for the sisters to wear to Midnight
mass; instead those without wore their bed covers.

## JOINING THE ORDER

When Mother Teresa first established the Missionaries of Charity, she
worked hard to help prepare the young women who entered the order. Father Van Exem and Father Henry also helped instruct the newcomers in
preparation for their lives as nuns. Gradually, these tasks became more the
duties of senior nuns. Mother Teresa always emphasized that the work of
a Missionary of Charity was no different from that of social workers. This
is not completely true; social workers, while working with the disadvan-
taged, often try to help correct the social ills that cause poverty in the first

place. For Mother Teresa and her nuns, living among the poor and living like the poor was a means to find God and bear witness to his presence and his will.

Women who apply to join the order must meet four requirements. They must be physically and mentally healthy. They must have the ability and the desire to learn. Common sense is a necessity as is a cheerful disposition; they would need all they could muster in working with the poor. Initially, women enter the order for only a few weeks or months; in this way, they can see if they are truly meant to become a Missionary of Charity. As in other religious vocations, some find the life too dismal or too hard. Others decide to leave and marry. Women who choose to remain do so with the understanding that they will sever ties with their families. Rarely are they allowed to return home, though periodic visits are allowed every 10 years or so; in the case of a family illness, permission is given for the sister to go home. Often, if the nun is to be sent to a mission abroad, she is allowed to visit family members before leaving.

When joining the order, a young woman spends the first six months as an aspirant and the following six months as a postulant. This period also offers an opportunity for those who wish to leave to do so. The next two years are spent as a novitiate; again if one chooses to leave the order, she may do so without receiving special permission. At the end of the two-year period, the novitiates take their first vows. The next five years are known as the juniorate; from then on, each year the candidates renew their vows in order to strengthen their spiritual commitment to God and the order. For those wishing to leave, special permission is now required from the head of the order. The sixth year is known as the tertianship; before taking their final vows, the nuns are sent home to visit with their families and to reflect upon whether they are ready to assume the duties and life of a Missionary of Charity. When asked once about what she expected of her nuns, Mother Teresa replied:

> Let God radiate and live His life in her and through her in the slums. Let the sick and suffering find in her a real angel of comfort and consolation. Let her be the friend of the little children in the street.... I would much rather they make mistakes in kindness than work miracles in unkindness.[2]

## LIFE AT MOTHERHOUSE

The daily routine for those who chose to be Missionaries of Charity was long and grueling. Weekdays, the sisters rose at 4:40 A.M. to the call of

*Benedicamus Domino* ("Let us bless the Lord") and the response of *Deo Gratias* ("Thanks be to God"). Dressing at their bedsides with a sheet covering their heads, they went downstairs to wash their faces with water that came from the courtyard tank and was carried in empty powdered milk cans. They then collected ash from the kitchen stove to clean their teeth. Each sister washed herself with a small bit of soap; this same bit of soap was used to wash their clothes as well. Between 5:15 A.M. and 6:45 A.M. the sisters went for morning prayers, meditation, and then mass. They then went to the dining hall where each drank a glass of water before breakfast. In the beginning, there was no tea for breakfast; instead milk made from American powdered milk was given. Breakfast consisted of five *chapattis* (homemade bread made from wheat or other grain flours and baked without yeast) spread with clarified butter (*ghee*). The *chapattis* provided strength and energy to the body and it was required that all eat their allotment, something that many had a harder time doing than going without food. Father Henry once told a story of how, when the first newcomers joined the order, they came with the expectation that food would be insufficient and one of many deprivations they would suffer. At their first meal, Mother Teresa put their plates before each one. Amazed, the women looked at the plates full of food. They were told to eat it, as it was their due. Mother Teresa then reminded them that God "wants obedience rather than victims."[3] In addition to their food, all of the residents took a vitamin pill with their meal. After their quick breakfast, the sisters were out on the streets by 7:45 A.M. to begin their work. The sisters made a point of traveling together in pairs for their own safety as well as to help one another.

In the parlor of the Motherhouse is a hand-drawn chart that lists the various activities the sisters are to do. These included providing child welfare and educational programs and operating nutritional daycares; family planning centers; dispensaries; leprosy clinics; rehabilitation centers; shelters for the homeless, crippled and mentally disabled; homes for unwed mothers; and hospices for the sick and the dying. A separate column notes the total number of these institutions and the number of people who benefited from them. A world map with red pins denoted the areas where the Missionaries of Charity established homes or foundations. In time, Missionaries of Charity in Western Europe and the United States offered family visits and a prison ministry. The Missionaries of Charity's emphasis in India and many Third World countries—besides helping to educate the poor and tend the dying—came to be on homes for alcoholics, shelters for the homeless, soup kitchens, and hospices for AIDS patients.

By noontime, many sisters returned to Motherhouse for prayers and a midday meal, which consisted of five ladles of bulgur wheat and three bits of meat if there was any available. After the meal, housework was attended to and then came a rest of 30 minutes. Afterward, there was more prayer and afternoon tea at which the nuns ate two dry *chapattis*. There followed another half-hour of spiritual reading and instruction from Mother Teresa. The sisters then returned to the city.

By 6 in the evening, the sisters returned to the Motherhouse for prayers and dinner, which usually consisted of rice, *dhal* (a spicy dish made with lentils), tomatoes, onions and various seasonings, and other vegetables. During the meal, there was also 10 minutes of spiritual readings. After dinner, attention was given to darning and mending, using a razor blade, needle, and darning thread kept in a cigarette tin. There was also time for recreation; this was the one time that conversation about subjects other than work was permitted. The signal for this recreational conversation to begin was *Laudetur Jesus Christus* ("Praise be Jesus Christ"), to which the sisters answered "Amen." Now was the time that all could share what happened to them during the day. Then at 10 o'clock, the day was over; and everyone retired for the night.

Because Sundays were often as busy as weekdays, Mother Teresa set aside Thursdays as days of respite for the residents of Motherhouse. On this day, the sisters might engage in prayer and meditation. Quite often in the early days, Mother Teresa would take her group to the home of a Calcutta doctor, where they would have a picnic and relax on the grounds.

The physical demands of the sisters' work were strenuous. On any given day, they might have to jump railway tracks or ditches or slog through pools of standing water. During the rainy seasons, there was the danger of being caught in a flash flood. Mother Teresa instructed her nuns always to say their rosaries that each sister carried with her. In time, measuring distances covered was not added up in miles, but in how many rosaries were said. When the conditions they encountered were desperate or terrible, the Sisters sang High Mass in Latin.

Even with the emphasis on poverty, there were times when the sisters went without necessities. When there was no fuel to cook their meals, the sisters ate raw wheat that had been soaked overnight. When their curry was too bitter and there was nothing available to improve its taste, the sisters ate it for the sake of the conversion to Catholicism of the Mau Mau tribe in Africa. No matter the sacrifice, the sisters did it willingly and often with smiles on their faces.

Not all welcomed Mother Teresa and the Missionaries of Charity into their lives. Some of the poor resisted the sisters' efforts to help them, seeing them as trying to convert the poor to Catholicism. Others simply did not want charity. For those young women who offered their lives in service to the poor, rejection also waited. Many girls' families were ashamed of their vocation to help the poor and outcasts of the city. In some cases, family members, if coming upon a daughter or sister who had become a Missionary of Charity, crossed the streets or turned away to avoid looking at them. Many parents urged their daughters to leave and were often disappointed and surprised to hear their advice rejected.

## THE JOY OF BEING POOR

Throughout the early years of her congregation's existence, Mother Teresa continued to work hard. Up before any of her nuns and often toiling long after they had gone to bed, she never ceased to work. There was always something to do, whether it was persuading those with much to part with some of their goods, overseeing the everyday activities of the Motherhouse, or writing a history of the congregation. She appeared tireless, full of good cheer and ready to move on to the next task. For members of her congregation, she was nothing short of a marvel. As one sister explained, it was as if the constitution of the congregation was being acted out before their eyes. Mother Teresa exemplified for the order the joy of being poor, working hard, and having strong faith in God's providence.

No task was too menial or disgusting for Mother Teresa to undertake. One sister, repelled at the thought of cleaning the toilet, hid herself away. Mother Teresa passed by, not noticing the Sister in the hall. Seeing the state of the toilet, she immediately rolled up her sleeves and cleaned the toilet herself. The sister never forgot the experience and applied herself more fully to her tasks.

From all the sisters, Mother Teresa asked obedience. Those unable to eat the allotted five *chapattis* a day were not considered Missionaries of Charity material and were asked to leave. Other requirements of the order included speaking English at all times. Those who came to the order without finishing their studies were to complete them in addition to their work at the Motherhouse.

The nuns made other sacrifices in the face of cultural taboos. For instance, realizing that the congregation needed people with medical training, Mother Teresa asked some of the first sisters to earn medical degrees even though studying medicine meant mixing with men under conditions of unacceptable intimacy. Nevertheless, the women did as they were asked even though it meant being further ostracized from their families and cultural traditions.

Mother Teresa asked nothing of others that she would not do herself. She worked with her sisters and was protective of their well being. She also continued to trust that God would meet the needs of the congregation. This faith and devotion to God often rewarded Mother Teresa and her sisters in amazing ways. On one occasion when there was no food in the house, a knock came at the door. A woman standing outside had with her bags of rice. She later told Mother Teresa that she did not have any intention of going there, but for some reason came bringing the rice. That evening, Mother Teresa and the sisters had their dinner.

In another instance, Father Henry asked Mother Teresa for some money to print some leaflets. She searched the house and found only two rupees, which she gladly turned over to Father Henry. As he was leaving, he remembered a letter that he had brought for her. Opening it, Mother Teresa discovered a gift of 100 rupees. When a newcomer arrived at the Motherhouse, there was no pillow available for her; Mother Teresa offered the young woman hers, but the sisters refused to allow it, stating that she needed the pillow for her own rest. Mother Teresa insisted and while doing so, an Englishman appeared at the Motherhouse with a mattress. He was leaving the country and wanted to know if the sisters would have any use for his mattress. This and other events demonstrated to Mother Teresa the power of faith as well as God's providence when people completely surrendered their lives into his care.

As the sisters soon learned, there was great joy to be had from small things when living the life of the poor. One of the first Christmas holidays celebrated by the group was an example. One sister recalled how on Christmas morning the sisters awoke to find that the dining area had been decorated with streamers and balloons; by each place at the table was a white paper bag with a sister's name on it. Inside of each bag were letters from home and gifts from Mother Teresa. All the sisters received pencils; one remembered gifts of a bar of soap, a clothes peg, St. Christopher and Miraculous Medals, sweets, and a balloon. The sister remembered how thrilled she was by the gifts and Mother Teresa's generosity toward her congregation.

## REACHING OUT

By 1953, the work of the Missionaries of Charity had grown tremendously. On April 12, 1953, the initial group of Missionary Sisters took their first vows in Calcutta's Roman Catholic Cathedral; during the same ceremony, Mother Teresa took her final vows as a Missionary of Charity. She also now succeeded Archbishop Périer as superior of the order she had founded. Despite his early resistance to Mother Teresa's efforts, the archbishop had demonstrated his full support in the order's early years, believing, as many others did, that God's hand clearly was at work in his city.

In time, Mother Teresa and her sisters became a familiar sight in the streets of Calcutta. As news of their endeavors spread, Mother Teresa was asked on occasion to speak about her work. As a result, many groups and organizations pledged their aid to carry out the work of the Missionaries of Charity. It took time, but soon doctors, nurses, and other lay people were volunteering their time and skills to help Calcutta's poor. As the number of volunteer medical personnel increased, so did the number of dispensaries to help tend to the sick and dying. Mother Teresa was also able to increase the number of schools in the slum areas; with more teachers, more poor children had the opportunity to learn how to read and write. Even the City of Calcutta eventually relented: whenever there were 100 pupils studying with the Missionaries of Charity in one area, the city agreed to build a small school building for them.

Despite these strides, Mother Teresa felt that still she and her congregation were not doing enough to help the growing numbers of poor. In the wake of Indian independence, conditions had worsened throughout India and particularly in Calcutta. Malnutrition and overcrowded living conditions contributed to even more illness and suffering. Even the governing body of the city, the Calcutta Corporation, was powerless to help.

In the 3,000 official slums in the city, there resided more than two million persons. The overcrowded conditions forced many to seek shelter on railway platforms, in alleyways, or on city streets. Prisons were overflowing and hospitals had to turn away people because they had no room. Even with the help of relief organizations, the city struggled to take care of the problem. As a result, the sick and the starving, weakened by disease and hunger, simply dropped wherever they were to die. To many, Mother Teresa and her nuns were but a small trickle of hope in a growing sea of suffering.

## THE MISSIONARY OF CHARITY WAY

Confronted with the changes that the Roman Catholic Church faced as a result of Pope John XXIII's Second Vatican Council from 1962 to 1965, many of the Church's religious orders struggled to find their place in the changing world. The pope's goal was to revitalize the church, and he believed that changes in the liturgy and in some of the rules governing religious orders would make an effective beginning. However, in the wake of the Second Vatican Council, many religious orders not only implemented changes, but tried to make the religious vocations more meaningful and pertinent to keep in step with the twentieth century. Not everyone welcomed these changes; some orders preferred the old ways.

Beginning in the 1970s, many religious orders underwent dramatic transformations as the Catholic Church struggled to become more modern and accessible to its followers. For some women's religious congregations, these changes meant modifying the nun's habit, and in some cases completely forgoing it. Many nuns believed that if one was to be of genuine service in the world, then one must wear the clothes of the real world. Others believed that by leaving behind their religious habit, which was often viewed as a barrier to working with the public, they would make people feel more comfortable around them. The practice of doing away with the religious uniform also encouraged individuality among the order's nuns, and hopefully along with it, one's particular talents. Others eased their rules in order to attract potential applicants to their order, especially those women with backgrounds in social services, medicine, or other advanced degrees.

However, in the case of the Missionaries of Charity, Mother Teresa made virtually no concessions; even today, the order continues to attract many young women who wish to take the vows of extreme poverty and give their lives over to the service of the poor. Everything about the life of a Missionary of Charity emphasizes the long-held ideal of caring femininity; that is, the traditional role of women as caretakers subservient to men. It is an ideal that also asks one to suppress one's own will for the common good. The image is a particularly potent one in Western culture, where a woman in a nun's habit ministering to the needs of the ill and poor is seen as the epitome of female selflessness, despite the efforts of the modern-day women's movement to counteract this image.

Even the manner in which Mother Teresa spoke of her order reinforced this ideal. To Mother Teresa, she and her nuns were the wives of Christ crucified, their bond to God like a mystical marriage; she described the love that the Missionaries of Charity professed for Jesus in terms similar to the love between husband and wife. This is an even more dramatic contrast to the thinking of many of today's religious orders, who find the notion of a nun as a bride of Christ not only outdated, but ridiculous.

In establishing the Missionaries of Charity, Mother Teresa also made it clear that she would brook no interference from priests, or meddling, no matter how well-intentioned, from outsiders. She also deflected any advice about how to teach her nuns. This rigid sense of control has had some impact on the order. Although one can understand the decision not to have televisions in the homes of monastics, it was harder for outsiders to understand the absence of newspapers or magazines; in fact, there is little in the way of reading material at any of the homes. Being informed about world events, Mother Teresa thought, was a distraction. She preferred to put her trust in God, who would make known to her all that she needed to know. What books were available for the nuns tended to be of a religious nature, such as books on piety or the lives of the saints. Except for the nuns who became medical doctors, Mother Teresa did not want her sisters to be any better informed or educated than those they were trying to serve, a startling contrast to orders that encouraged their members to seek advanced college degrees or specialized training.

This practice drew a great deal of criticism from within the Church. Some officials believe that education is necessary, not just the knowledge of theology but also of secular disciplines. Mother Teresa's attitude toward education is especially puzzling since she herself valued education. Perhaps she came to regard education, like wealth and worldly goods, as a source of vanity that the devout ought to sacrifice to the glory of the Lord.

Mother Teresa left her imprint on almost every aspect of the order. The old-fashioned discipline and rigid obedience required was and is today, more than some can bear. Some did not like being told what to do all the time. Others felt that even as the women grew older and more senior in the order's hierarchy, they were often forced to maintain a student-teacher relationship with Mother Teresa. For many, that clearly was no longer appropriate and had the effect of preventing the women from growing up. Some even felt uncomfortable using the term "Mother" as it denoted a childish dependence on Mother Teresa, which she encouraged.

Others, though, found themselves drawn to the Missionaries of Charity precisely because they did not have to grow up and make difficult decisions that adulthood requires. The black-and-white life of the order is such that those who are immature will have an easier time coping with its rigors than those who are prone to questioning and learning. This is in contrast to what was taking place in other orders, as rules became more relaxed and nuns allowed to make more of their own decisions. The reforms of Vatican Council II, ironically, also contributed to a drop in vocations. In 1990, the number of women in religious orders had dropped by more than half, from a record high of almost a million women serving as nuns in 1970. Today, third-world vocations continue to increase, while in the West, the numbers continue to decline.

## THE INCULTURATION OF POVERTY

One of the greatest challenges that faced Mother Teresa, and that continues today, was the difficult balance of realism and idealism. In some cases, the Missionaries of Charity, in their zeal to serve the poor, have made some questionable choices. In one instance the sisters removed a radiator from a house because the poor had no heat in their homes. According to a nun who is a member of the Sisters of Sion, the act was

> patronizing to the poor. . . . We are learning from the poor, the way we should respond to the poor is that we are in this together. Some of us are emotionally poor or poor in education. Of course you can deprive yourself but I have had the opportunities of a good education, there I'm a rich person; we must recognize that and not play at being poor. You can live alongside the poor but you must also be realistic.[4]

While Mother Teresa and her nuns adapted to life among the poor in India and later in other Third World countries, when it came time to establish homes in the West, the order often faced a different set of circumstances. To what extent should the order inculturate, that is adapt to the culture of the poor in the West, which is often very different from that in the third world. For instance, in establishing a shelter for women in the United States, did the sisters have an obligation to make sure that the women they helped not only received housing and meals, but also help to navigate the extensive red tape of the various social agencies to find aid, jobs, or other support services? The Missionaries of Charity would say no; that their vows do not extend to doing this type of work. However, there are those in the Church who would come to feel otherwise.

In one instance, Mother Teresa's rigorous attitude toward austerity for her order made headlines. In San Francisco, the order was given a former convent. When Mother Teresa arrived at the house, she was very unhappy, telling the bishop that the house was too big and elegant for their purposes. As a result, the mattresses, carpets, and many pieces of furniture were thrown out of the house into the street. A boiler that provided hot water was also taken out. Some in the order believed the matter could have been taken care of more discreetly and were unhappy at the ruckus the incident caused. On another occasion, Mother Teresa scolded her nuns for storing some canned tomatoes. She lectured them, reminding them that the order did not store food, but relied on God to provide for them.

## A HOLISTIC WHOLE

The theology that Mother Teresa followed is rooted in Church teach-ings prior to Vatican II. This doctrine emphasizes the spirit over the flesh; as such, it is the spirit that must be taken care of first. This attitude stressed the glory of suffering, as the human body was often identified as weak and sinful. Modern Catholic theologians have modified this view and speak of the importance of good health for both body and soul. Glo-rified suffering serves no purpose and is thought to be an evil in which no good is found. To suffer is only good if there is a purpose and the possibil-ity of turning it into something worthwhile.

For Mother Teresa, by contrast, suffering was the expected path one must travel in order to reach heaven. This attitude helps explain how such places as Nirmal Hriday, which became the home for the dying, would be run. In caring to the very ill and dying, Mother Teresa was draw-ing on the traditional practice of offering solace and comfort instead of medical aid. This practice dates from the medieval period when religious orders ran hospices for pilgrims or sanctuaries for the poor. There was, at best, limited medical care available; what the sisters did in these places was help to prepare the dying person's soul for heaven.

By the nineteenth century, this attitude underwent a dramatic trans-formation with sisters such as Mother Mary Aikenhead, founder of the Irish Sisters of Charity, whose work helped lay the foundation for the modern hospice movement. There were others too such as Dame Cicely Saunders or Sister Frances Dominica, who helped change the way that re-ligious orders treated the seriously ill and dying. Their work is often over-shadowed by Mother Teresa and the Missionaries of Charity, whom many in the West believe had done the most to transform the way the dying are cared for. In India and other Third World countries, there is little choice in how one dies. Because of that, Mother Teresa's work had been elevated and in some cases misunderstood. It was an approach that would make her an easy target in later years.

But for now, many of these criticisms were far in the future. Clearly, the Missionaries of Charity had struck a resounding chord within the Cal-cutta community. For Mother Teresa, there was still much to do. She and her order had only just begun their work.

## NOTES

1. Kathryn Spink, *Mother Teresa* (San Francisco: Harper & Row, 1997), p. 44.

2. Raghu Rai and Navin Chawla, *Faith and Compassion: The Life and Work of Mother Teresa* (Rockport, Mass.: Element, 1999), p. 47.

3. Edward Le Joly, *Mother Teresa of Calcutta: A Biography* (San Francisco: Harper & Row, 1977), p. 23.

4. Anne Sebba, *Mother Teresa: Beyond the Image* (New York: Doubleday, 1997), p. 169.

*Mother Teresa and Pope John Paul II ride in his popemobile, Calcutta, 1986. AP/Wide World Photos.*

*Mother Teresa stands on the balcony of her residence and listens as the nuns from her Missionaries of Charity sing her "Happy Birthday" in Calcutta, August 26, 1990. AP/Wide World Photos.*

*Mother Teresa with documentary filmmakers Ann Petrie and Jeanette Petrie, who made* Mother Teresa: The Legacy, *which premiered at her beatification. Photofest.*

*Statue of Mother Teresa after it was unveiled in Skopje, Macedonia, September 5, 1999. AP/Wide World Photos.*

# Chapter 6

# KALIGHAT

On a rainy day in 1952, a young boy, no more than 13 or 14 years old, lay dying on a neighborhood street. He appeared to be one of the many beggar children who are found in the streets of Calcutta. Naked and emaciated, the boy's limbs looked more like matchsticks than arms or legs. A concerned resident called the ambulance, which took the boy to a nearby hospital. The hospital, already overcrowded, refused to help. Instead, the boy was dumped in a Calcutta street gutter where he died alone and unknown. At some point the city sent a van or a cart to haul the body away. Although such scenes were common in Calcutta, a local newspaper picked up the story of the dead boy and heightened public attention to the dying poor.

Mother Teresa was no stranger to the problem. In the increasing number of talks she gave to the public about her congregation, she related a very similar story. One day, when she and another sister were just beginning their work, they encountered what appeared to be a bundle of rags lying on a street. As they approached, they realized, to their horror, that the bundle was not just rags, but a middle-aged woman, half-conscious, her face half-eaten away by rats and ants.

Together, Mother Teresa and her companion carried the woman to the nearest hospital. The nurses refused to take the woman, claiming the hospital had no beds. When Mother Teresa asked hospital officials where she could go, they told her to take the woman back where she had found her. Frustrated, Mother Teresa refused to leave until she had a promise that the hospital would make room for the sick woman. In the end, hospital authorities relented and gave the dying woman a mattress on the floor.

She died a few hours later with Mother Teresa by her side. It was then, Mother Teresa told her audiences, that she had decided to find a place for the dying and take care of them herself.

## ASKING ONLY FOR A PLACE

"When Mother Teresa began her work in the slums," recalled one sister, "we often found people dying or sometimes dead."[1] When possible, the sisters took the ailing person to the hospital, where more often than not they were turned away. Often there was no place to take them at all, leaving the sisters unable to offer anything else except comfort and company until the person died. At one point, Mother Teresa rented two rooms for five rupees each in the Motijihl slum. But the space, only eight feet square, could not even begin to hold the numbers of dying people who needed help; at best only two to three persons could be accommodated, leaving little room for the sisters to tend to them. When one of the patients died during the night, the others, now fearful, fled. Undaunted, the sisters continued to bring the sick and dying to the two rooms, while praying that they could find a larger building adequate to their needs.

Mother Teresa also realized that, if she were to realize her goal of establishing a home for the dying, then she needed more than prayers. Determined, she went to the city's Chief Medical Officer, Dr. Ahmed. Explaining her desire to him, Mother Teresa promised that if he would help her find a place, she would do the rest. The doctor, well aware of Mother Teresa's growing reputation, treated her request seriously. By offering to help, Mother Teresa and her nuns would be relieving some of the already heavy burden the city faced in dealing with dying people on the streets.

In fact, Dr. Ahmed knew of a place that might perfectly suit Mother Teresa's needs. Together they went to inspect a building, which had been used as a pilgrim's hostel near the Temple of Kali, the Hindu goddess of death and fertility. Located in the Kalighat district, the temple was situated near the banks of the Hooghly River. The site was popular among the Hindus who came to worship at the temple. According to legend, Kali's father made a sacrifice in order to guarantee the birth of a son. Unfortunately, the gift did not include an offering to Shiva, Kali's husband. Insulted by the slight to her husband, Kali committed suicide. Shiva, desolate over the death of his wife, carried her in his arms, threatening destruction wherever he went. To save mankind, another god, Vishnu, hurled a discus at Kali's corpse. The body shattered, falling in pieces to the ground, which is now considered sacred.

Of all the consecrated ground, the most sacred was the area where the toes of Kali's right foot lay. On that spot, a temple to the goddess was built. Over time, the temple was surrounded by streets bearing pictures of the deity and became an important and symbolic center of worship for Hindus throughout India. Some came to fulfill a vow; others journeyed seeking cure for an illness. Still others came to celebrate important ceremonies such as naming rites for infants, marriages, or cremations on one of the funeral pyres located near the temple. The religious importance of the temple of Kali was so great that many Hindus wished to be cremated there.

The building that Dr. Ahmed showed Mother Teresa consisted of two great rooms set at right angles and linked by a passageway. Calcutta officials had received complaints that squatters were misusing the building, and so wished to have someone occupy it to save it from further destruction. Besides the large, airy rooms, there was also electricity, gas for cooking, and a large enclosed courtyard where patients could take the air and sun and where clothes and bedding could be hung to dry. Mother Teresa decided on the spot that she would accept the building; the doctor, acting on behalf of the city, agreed to let her have it provisionally. When asked later why she accepted the doctor's offer, she explained that since the building was associated with the famous Hindu temple and that pilgrims used to come to rest there, so would the dying before continuing their final journey to heaven. Almost immediately, Mother Teresa and several of her nuns and novitiates set to work. The quarters had fallen into terrible condition and needed to be cleaned from top to bottom to make them ready for the new arrivals.

## NIRMAL HRIDAY

On August 22, 1952, the pilgrim's hostel opened under the name Nirmal Hriday, which is Bengali for Pure or Immaculate Heart. Since it opened on the day that celebrates the Virgin's Immaculate Heart, the building was named in her honor. To make ready for the patients, the nuns had placed low cots and mattresses on ledges in both the large rooms, which, when filled to capacity, would hold 30 men in one room and 30 women in another. But Mother Teresa and her helpers did not have much time to contemplate this latest offering from Providence. They soon took to the streets in search of the hopelessly ill and suffering who had no place to go.

Early on, Mother Teresa laid down some rules for Nirmal Hriday. No leprosy patients would be admitted. This was done to allay the fears of other patients who might refuse to come or try to leave. Mother Teresa also instituted these rules to calm the fears of the local residents and pilgrims who lived near or worshipped at the temple. It was implicitly understood that people from all religious creeds and races would be welcome at Nirmal Hriday. Mother Teresa also decided that only patients refused by city hospitals, of whom there were many, would be admitted. Soon, city ambulances made their way to the doors of Nirmal Hriday to deliver patients whom the city's hospitals had rejected. But Mother Teresa and the other nuns continued to search the streets for the ill and dying, whom they transported to the home in a wheelbarrow.

Those brought to Nirmal Hriday were given medical treatment whenever possible. Patients who were beyond saving received the last rites according to their faith; for Hindus, this meant water from the nearby Ganges on their lips; for the followers of Islam, readings from the Koran (the Islamic holy book); for those who were Catholic, confession and communion. While recovery from their ailments was cause for thankfulness, the primary goal of Nirmal Hriday was to offer those who were dying a chance to pass away in peace and dignity. As Mother Teresa once stated, "A beautiful death is for people who lived like animals to die like angels— loved and wanted."[2]

## A MISSION UNDER FIRE

Not everyone was pleased about the creation of Nirmal Hriday. Although Mother Teresa believed the hostel's proximity to the shrine was beneficial for the dying, residents of the area as well as visitors to the shrine, felt differently. Many believed that having a home for the dying nearby defiled the temple grounds. As Father Van Exem remembered, the situation was full of bitter irony. Even though the home for the dying was near a temple honoring a deity of death, "people did not want the dying to come there actually to die."[3] Many days, Mother Teresa and her nuns faced angry demonstrators shouting at them to leave. On several occasions, protestors threw stones at the nuns. There were even death threats made against the Missionaries of Charity and Mother Teresa. A man once threatened to kill Mother Teresa as she was making her way to the home. She did not move and told the man that if he killed her, she would only reach God sooner. The man let her pass.

Other Hindus complained that in tending to Hindu patients, Mother Teresa and her nuns were also trying to convert the dying to Christianity. The Brahmins (upper-class Indians), who served as temple priests, wrote regularly to the city of Calcutta, complaining about Nirmal Hriday, asking the city to evict the tenants. They argued that the agreement made with Mother Teresa was only provisional, and that she and her patients be removed from the area as soon as possible.

Finally, Dr. Ahmed, accompanied by a police officer, went to Nirmal Hriday to see for themselves what was really going on. As they entered the building, they saw Mother Teresa pulling maggots from the flesh of a patient. The stench was so overwhelming that the two men could barely stay in the room. Dr. Ahmed heard Mother Teresa telling the dying patient to say a prayer from his religion and she would say a prayer from hers. Together, she said, they both have offered something beautiful to God. When she turned and saw the two men, she offered to show them around the home. The police officer, with tears in his eyes, said no, that there was no need to see anything else. Upon returning to the demonstrating crowd outside, the policeman spoke and said that he would remove Mother Teresa from the premises, but only if the women of the neighborhood came in to continue her work. Although the visit from Dr. Ahmed soothed the situation somewhat, hostility remained toward the home and the nuns, especially from the Brahmin priests, who continued to petition the city to remove Mother Teresa, her nuns, and the patients from the hostel.

Then, one day, a young priest at the temple, who had been one of Mother Teresa's most vocal critics, fell ill. Vomiting blood, he was diagnosed with the last stages of tuberculosis. No hospital would admit him, and so it was that he came to Nirmal Hriday to die. He was given a place in a corner and the nuns lovingly tended him. He died not long afterward. When the other Brahmin priests learned what had happened and how he had been treated by the Missionaries of Charity, their hostilities subsided. They realized then what others were learning too: the nuns at Nirmal Hriday took care of all who came with a love and tenderness and asked for nothing in return.

## LIFE AT NIRMAL HRIDAY

Like the Motherhouse on Lower Circular Road, daily life at Nirmal Hriday had a routine all its own. Anyone could enter Nirmal Hriday just by walking through the door. The large open rooms remained divided into two wards: one for men, the other for women. A simple board hung in the hall listing the number of men and women currently being treated at Nirmal Hriday. In the beginning, the dying were laid on the black marble floor. Soon, though, each room contained three rows of low iron beds, with two rows resting on a raised platform. Behind each bed a number was painted on the wall to help keep count of patients and beds. Patients who needed fluids had intravenous tubes connected to various bottles. Those patients who were dying were placed near the entrance of each ward, so the sisters could better tend them. Nirmal Hriday was quiet, too, with the only sounds coming from the sisters moving about or a medical treatment being administered. At one end of the hall was a burlap curtain; behind this, the dead were kept until it was time for burial. In many cases, after a patient died, local religious groups representing the Islamic, Hindu, or Christian communities claimed the bodies in order to bury the deceased according to his or her religious beliefs.

From the day Nirmal Hriday opened, Mother Teresa kept a meticulous record of the number of cases admitted. Upon admittance, each patient's name, age, and address were recorded; whether the patient died or was released was also recorded. For those with no name or home, the entry was labeled "Unknown" with the date of admittance recorded. Over the years, with the aid of better hygiene and nutrition among the population and the construction of more hospitals and clinics tending to the poor, Nirmal Hriday saw its mortality rate drop from almost 50 percent to 10 percent.

As word of Nirmal Hriday spread, volunteers came forward to aid Mother Teresa and the Missionaries of Charity in their work. Hindu pilgrims who came to worship at the temple now made contributions to Nirmal Hriday. A local businessman sent a delivery boy every month with a supply of Indian cigarettes known as *bidis* to give to the patients, and in time decided to deliver them himself. On Sundays, some of the wealthy members of Calcutta society came to Nirmal Hriday to wash and shave the patients. Other volunteers came to help clean out wounds, cut hair, or feed the patients. Still others cleaned the rooms, washing floors by hand with a mixture of water, ashes, and disinfectant. Almost all who visited left Nirmal Hriday transformed. For Mother Teresa, such experiences were necessary to understanding the plight of the poor. "Don't just look around like a spectator," she said to newcomers, "really look with your ears and your eyes, and you will be shown what you can do to help."[4]

Mother Teresa also instituted a rule that everyone from novitiate to nun work at Nirmal Hriday. It was backbreaking work as one had to be doctor, nurse, porter, and attendant at any given time. The hours were long, usually extending far beyond the normal workday with 18-hour days a common occurrence. There was little respite, for there always was medicine to be given, patients to be washed or fed, or prayers to be said. A sense of humor helped to counter relentless suffering and death. But few Sisters complained; more startling perhaps, many Missionaries of Charity asked to work at Nirmal Hriday.

## AN ONGOING MISSION

Despite all she had done, there was residual anger over Mother Teresa's presence so near a Hindu temple. One Calcutta city council member introduced a motion that called for moving the home to a more suitable location. City leaders debated the issue and then agreed that, as soon as a suitable location was found for Nirmal Hriday, the facility would be moved. As most officials were happy with what Mother Teresa was doing, however, they tended to downplay complaints. And since they did not want Mother Teresa to leave, no one even proposed an alternate location for Nirmal Hriday, which continues to operate in the same location even today.

Most patients at Nirmal Hriday fell into two categories: street cases, or people who had no family and were destitute, and family cases, where family members were unwilling or unable to care for those, especially the elderly, who were sick. In family cases, if the elderly patient recovered, the sisters made every effort to reunite the family members. Later on, those patients abandoned by their families were transferred to Prem Dan, a home established in 1975 for the elderly poor, and those ill but with a good chance of recovery. No matter the distinctions, the sisters tried never to turn anyone away who was in need.

Since it first opened in 1952, Nirmal Hriday has rescued more than 54,000 persons from the street. Of that number, half died at the home. Although a mortality rate of 50 percent is high, Nirmal Hriday was a home for the dying. In this respect, Mother Teresa and the Missionaries of Charity succeeded in their mission to provide a sanctuary for those with nowhere else to go to make their peace with God and to die with dignity. The home also emerged as one of the most potent symbols in the West for Mother Teresa and her work. As she later wrote, "In my heart, I carry the last glances of the dying. I do all I can so that they feel loved at that most important moment when a seemingly useless existence can be redeemed."[5]

## EARLY CRITICS

No sooner had the criticism of Nirmal Hriday died down, then rumblings about Mother Teresa herself surfaced. These criticisms grew throughout the decade and followed her for years. As the number of Mother Teresa's detractors increased, the debate about her character and her attitudes toward such controversial topics as abortion and family planning intensified. As donations to her order increased, Mother Teresa came under scrutiny for accepting contributions from questionable donors.

One of the first to question Mother Teresa's handling of Nirmal Hriday was a young medical student named Marcus Fernandes. Before coming to Nirmal Hriday, Fernandes was already familiar with Mother Teresa and her work. His sister had attended Loreto, and through her, he had learned a great deal about the Missionaries of Charity.

As inexperienced at medicine as he was, Fernandes, nonetheless, was unhappy with the haphazard clinical practices that he found at Nirmal Hriday. He made several suggestions to Mother Teresa about how she could improve the chances for patients' recoveries. According to Fernandes, the biggest problem at Nirmal Hriday was not cancer, tuberculosis, or heart ailments, but malnutrition. Fernandes suggested that giving patients rice fortified with vitamin supplements would improve their chances of survival. He also suggested new approaches to diagnosis along with a separate area where he could make a more thorough examination of patients. His recommendations failed to convince Mother Teresa. His widow, Patricia Fernandes, remarked, "He could not persuade her to treat them with vitamins. She did not want them treated; she expected people to die and would simply say, 'Well, she's gone to God.' She was not particularly interested in medicine."[6]

Others who visited or worked at Nirmal Hriday similarly noted Mother Teresa's seeming nonchalance over others' deaths. One visitor recalled how, when her sisters asked Mother Teresa to try to save a 16-year-old boy from dying, she simply blessed the ailing young man and said, "Never mind, it's a lovely day to go to Heaven."[7] A young woman volunteer, who had been thinking of joining the Missionaries of Charity, helped a young woman with a heart defect enter Nirmal Hriday. Mother Teresa told her that there was nothing more she could do, it was in God's hands as to whether the young woman would live or die.

Dr. Fernandes stayed at Nirmal Hriday for two years, before leaving for London to complete his medical training. When he returned to India and again offered his services to Mother Teresa he saw, to his dismay, that nothing had changed at Nirmal Hriday except that some conditions had become worse. A great deal of the money that had been donated to Nirmal Hriday was being wasted, and the facilities needed improvement. Fernandes was particularly angered by the sight of an X-ray machine that was now useless and rusting. When he approached Mother Teresa about it, she told him that there was no one trained to use it. Dr. Fernandes continued off and on to see Mother Teresa, but after her refusal to pay for his treatment of a skin ailment that had been plaguing her, he severed his association with her. He did, however, volunteer his time and services with other charity and missionary groups in Calcutta. But, when asked, he never changed his assessment of Mother Teresa. To him, she was a hard and extremely ruthless woman.[8]

Another vocal critic of Mother Teresa was a British doctor of ophthalmology, Major E. John Somerset, who was affiliated with the Calcutta Medical College Hospital from 1939 to 1961. During the early 1950s, when Mother Teresa and her Missionaries of Charity were first becoming known, Dr. Somerset was donating his time to five or six charitable homes for the aged and sick in Calcutta. He soon began getting regular visits from Mother Teresa, who would bring him patients she had found in need of treatment. Many of the cases Somerset treated were children who suffered from severe vitamin A deficiency to such a degree that their corneas were melting away. Although Somerset promised Mother Teresa that he would see as many cases as he could, he asked that she let him know beforehand and not come when he was seeing his regular patients. But to Somerset's dismay, Mother Teresa ignored his request and continued to bring patients to him without an appointment. He came to regard her as a nuisance and a bother.

Another volunteer, Sue Ryder, who had worked as a nurse during World War II, also had her problems with Mother Teresa. When Ryder came to India with her husband, she occasionally visited the slums with Mother Teresa. She approached Mother Teresa about merging the Missionaries of Charities ventures with her own charitable foundation, but was rebuffed. The two women had other problems with each other. Ryder strongly suggested that the night staff at Nirmal Hriday be increased, as it was often overnight that patients needed the most comfort and care. However, Mother Teresa refused to consider a change in schedules: her sisters were to return to the convent at night to say their prayers. The matter was closed.

## THE BRITISH, COLONIAL GUILT, AND MOTHER TERESA

Complaints about Mother Teresa did little to dampen the tremendous goodwill many felt toward her and her congregation. This was particularly true in the English Catholic community of Calcutta. Many women volunteered to help raise funds or provide toys, food, and clothing, especially for the children. One volunteer, an Englishwoman named Ann Blaikie, coordinated volunteer efforts and on occasion spoke to civic organizations and other groups about the Missionaries of Charity.

As Anne Sebba, one of Mother Teresa's biographers, noted, the attitude of the English, especially English women, was very important in

Mother Teresa's early successes. Many of these women lived in the exclusive areas of Calcutta, belonged to certain clubs, and socialized only with each other. Their only interaction with Bengalis came through their domestics or in some official capacity. Some British who spent time in India before and after its independence believe that Mother Teresa went a long way in helping them to justify the privileged life that many English living in India enjoyed. As more than one person recalled, by stepping out from their upper-class surroundings and journeying to the slums or to Nirmal Hriday or to one of the many clinics or schools Mother Teresa had established, they could, for a moment or two anyway, say that they helped Mother Teresa and eased their guilt. And Mother Teresa knew how to manipulate her audiences, whether she was speaking to one person or an entire roomful. One man who grew up knowing Mother Teresa described how she solicited funds and supplies. According to his account, Mother Teresa fixed her gaze on the person and stated how the Missionaries of Charity really needed such and such an item, and that they did not know how they would find the money. The person often found himself rooted to the spot; almost always that person ended up pulling out the checkbook to provide Mother Teresa with whatever she wanted.[9] Other English men and women who spent time in India and also helped Mother Teresa felt something much more profound. As one man explained it, when he was in India during the war, he rarely came into contact with poor people, though he realized he should have. He also believed that the British had taken far more out of India than they had contributed. In the end, the British failed in their duties to aid the poor and helpless of India.[10] Helping Mother Teresa was a way to make amends.

Although this attitude may have eased many consciences, it also angered the people who were the supposed beneficiaries of such generosity, who resented Western condescension. For many Indians, the efforts of Westerners, and the British in particular, promoted the false impression that the people of India were indifferent to the suffering of their own. Further, these critics charged, Westerners, as symbolized by Mother Teresa and the Missionaries of Charity, appeared to be the only ones who do help the poor and infirm in India, when in fact this was not the case.

Still, there is little question that with the establishment of Nirmal Hriday, Mother Teresa and the Missionaries of Charity gained a reputation for good works not only in Calcutta, but throughout the nation and the world. By 1955, though, Mother Teresa had other things on her mind. She turned her energies and attention to two groups who needed her help and for whom she had done nothing specific: children and lepers.

## NOTES

1. Raghu Rai and Navin Chawla, *Mother Teresa* (Rockport, Mass.: Element, 1992), p. 159.

2. Kathryn Spink, *Mother Teresa* (San Francisco: Harper & Row, 1997), p. 55.

3. Rai and Chawla, *Mother Teresa*, p. 160.

4. Spink, *Mother Teresa*, p. 57.

5. Mother Teresa with Jose Luis Gonzàles-Balado, *Mother Teresa: In My Own Words* (New York: Gramercy Books, 1996), p. 70.

6. Anne Sebba, *Mother Teresa: Beyond the Image* (New York: Doubleday, 1997), p. 60.

7. Sebba, *Mother Teresa*, p. 60.

8. Sebba, *Mother Teresa*, p. 61.

9. Sebba, *Mother Teresa*, p. 65.

10. Sebba, *Mother Teresa*, pp. 63–64.

# Chapter 7

# SHISHU BHAVAN AND SHANTINAGAR: PLACES OF PEACE

By 1955, Mother Teresa turned her energies to another group in need: the children of the poor. In a relatively short time, Mother Teresa and the Missionaries of Charity had made progress in providing education for poor children with the creation of schools in the slums. But providing children with an education paled beside even bigger problem: what to do with the growing number of unwanted and abandoned children in the city.

Since India's independence, the number of unwanted children roaming in the streets of Calcutta has increased. Orphaned, sick, and disabled children were often cast into the streets to fend for themselves. Some children tried to eke out a living by begging, others through petty crime such as stealing. Poor families, faced with the growing burden of supporting their children, abandoned them. Young girls and infants particularly were at great risk, because in Indian society boys are considered more valuable. Evidence of this cultural bias was everywhere; for the Missionaries of Charity the sight of a newborn female infant, alone and left to die, was common. For Mother Teresa, children were a special gift from God. She wrote:

> Children long for somebody to accept them, to love them, to praise them, to be proud of them. Let us bring the child back to the center of our care and concern. This is the only way the world can survive because our children are the only hope for the future. As older people are called to God, only their children can take their place.[1]

Even though many Catholic charities were active in this area and Calcutta had a number of orphanages, the number of children on the streets were growing too quickly for these groups to manage.

## SHISHU BHAVAN

To Mother Teresa, the sight of so many unloved children was heartbreaking. It was not enough to rescue as many children as possible from the streets, the gutters, the garbage heaps, and the alleyways. What was needed was a refuge where the children could be taken, nurtured, and loved. For Mother Teresa, these children were nothing less than a symbol of the Christ child. Although other charities in Calcutta did their best to deal with the problem, it was clear that they needed help. As with Nirmal Hriday, Mother Teresa had once again identified a problem that was causing the city officials of Calcutta a great deal of embarrassment. As a result of her previous successes, she received recognition and cooperation from the highest offices in the city.

During one of her many forays through the city, Mother Teresa made the acquaintance of Dr. B.C. Roy, Chief Minister of West Bengal and a medical doctor. Dr. Roy often gave free consultations at his home office and Mother Teresa lined up with the rest of the poor every day at 6 A.M. More often than not, her requests were political, rather than medical. She told the doctor about the needs for water or electricity in a slum area that she had visited. Dr. Roy dutifully wrote memos to the official responsible, informing him of the problem. In time, he began to pay closer attention to the tiny nun who showed such great concern for the poor of his city. He then told her to come to his office, where he helped open the doors of various city offices to her. Mother Teresa now could call on him freely; in turn, Dr. Roy trusted her completely. With his help, she began to implement her latest project for the children of the poor.

And so it was on September 23, 1955, Mother Teresa opened the first Shishu Bhavan, a home for children. Located near Creek Lane, and just a short walk from the Motherhouse, the small unpainted bungalow was the first of several children's homes established by the Missionaries of Charity. Like Nirmal Hriday, the sisters had to clean the house thoroughly to get it ready for its new occupants. Though the house was small, it opened into a spacious courtyard; Mother Teresa had rented the home from a Muslim who had left the city.

When the first Shishu Bhavan was ready, the sisters went about in search of residents. They did not have to look far; most everywhere they went, they found children in need, many of them infants, some not even a day old. The infants were brought back to the house, cleaned, fed, and given medical treatment, as many suffered from malnutrition and tuberculosis. Those that survived were dressed in green-and-white checked clothing, then placed in boxes, packing crates, or even on the floor. Those who were too sick were held lovingly by the sisters until they died. Like the home for the dying, Mother Teresa wanted these small infants and children to be cleansed, held, and loved, even though death was imminent. As crowded as the Shishu Bhavan was, Mother Teresa never turned away a child, even if it meant that infants slept three to a cot; for those fighting for their life, a box heated by a light bulb was used.

By 1958, the Missionaries of Charity had established Shishu Bhavans to care for more than 90 children. In addition, Mother Teresa accepted a government grant that provided 33 rupees for each child. But after a few months of working within the government guidelines, Mother Teresa decided to stop taking the grant money. She believed she could do just as well spending 17 rupees per child; this allowed her to take in more children and provide them with the care they needed.

Besides seeking out children themselves, the Missionaries of Charity also sent letters to all medical clinics and nursing homes in Calcutta, stating that they would welcome any child without a home. Periodically, young pregnant women, many of whom had been cast out of their homes, would show up at a Shishu Bhavan seeking refuge. The sisters took them in, and the expectant mothers worked in the homes until they gave birth. If for some reason the new mother could not care for her child, the sisters took the child, but only as a last resort. The home also acted as an afternoon high school for young boys who would otherwise have been on the streets learning to rob and steal.

## CARING FOR THE CHILDREN

As with many of her undertakings, Mother Teresa chose a practical approach in overseeing the Shishu Bhavans. She firmly believed in teaching the older children a skill or giving them a practical education that would allow them to make their way in the world. Among the first things she did when opening the home was to acquire some old typewriters. She taught some of the older girls how to type with the hope that they could find secretarial jobs. The sisters also taught carpentry for boys and needlework for girls. Because Mother Teresa's schools were not recognized by the government, nor would the Calcutta schools accept the children unless they paid tuition or fees, she depended on the largesse of benefactors to sponsor the children. One of the first was a wealthy Hindu woman who sponsored 10 children for 10 years.

In time, other donors would do the same. This practice helped the children to receive the education or technical skills they needed to become self-supporting. It was common, for instance, for an Indian donor to pay tuition for an infant from birth to the end of the child's school years. Over the years, the circle of donors widened considerably, as donors throughout the world sponsored children at the Shishu Bhavans. The support monies donated for the children were placed in a bank account until the child reached school age; the funds were then used to pay for the child's education. This system proved so successful that in 1975 Mother Teresa organized the World Child Welfare Fund, which shared the financial assistance among all of the children under the care of the Missionaries of Charity.

## THE PROMISE OF A NEW LIFE

For residents of Shishu Bhavan who were of marrying age, Mother Teresa, in accordance with Hindu custom, helped arrange marriages. Acting as a marriage broker, Mother Teresa worked with other Hindu families seeking a bride for a male relative. While the social status of the girls who lived at Shishu Bhavan was, in general, low, Mother Teresa made sure that each young woman had a dowry, or gifts, to present to the prospective bridegroom's family. These dowries always included a new sari, a few trinkets, and a wedding ring. Local benefactors also helped in many instances adding to the dowry some gold ornaments, household utensils, furniture, and in many cases, money in a small bank account opened in the future bride's name. On any given day, the couples could be found gathering outside the Motherhouse to greet Mother Teresa and her Missionaries of Charity. In time, a joke started to make the rounds that a prospective bridegroom had better watch his step as he was inheriting not one mother-in-law, but several.

Perhaps the most important program that Mother Teresa created for the children's homes were adoptions. When the program began, the majority of children were placed with Christian families. Slowly, many Hindu middle-class families opened their homes to unwanted and abandoned children. Initially, boys were still preferred over girls, but, over time, many Hindu families were happy to welcome a new child, regardless of sex, into their homes. Soon, Mother Teresa began to find homes for Indian children with overseas adoptive parents from Europe and North America. However, the majority of families wishing to adopt wanted only healthy children. Though physically disabled children might find a home with European families, children with severe mental disabilities stayed at the Shishu Bhavan.

In emphasizing adoption, Mother Teresa was also battling abortion, which she strongly opposed. She once wrote that with abortion:

> the mother kills even her own child to solve her problems. And, by abortion, the father is told he does not have to take any responsibility at all for the child he has brought into the world. That father is likely to put other women into the same trouble. So abortion leads to abortion. Any country that accepts abortion is not teaching its people to love but to use violence to get what they want.[2]

For Mother Teresa, adoption was the best way to combat not only abortion, but the growing practice of sterilizing women to cut down on escalating birth rates. The Indian government advocated female sterilization as a way to combat population growth. To combat abortion clinics, Mother Teresa and her sisters sent word to medical clinics, hospitals, and police stations that the Missionaries of Charity would accept all unwanted children.

In addition to adoption, Mother Teresa also became involved in family planning. The Missionaries began instruction in what Mother Teresa called Holy Family Planning, which emphasized natural family planning based on the rhythm method, the only family-planning practice sanctioned by the Roman Catholic Church. The Missionaries also set up a number of family-planning centers where young married couples not only learned how the rhythm method worked, but also learned that abstaining from sex was another way to avoid unwanted pregnancies. Despite the simplicity of these methods, teaching them to the poor had its drawbacks. One familiar story involved a woman who had already given birth to a large number of children. Wishing to avoid another pregnancy, she received instruction in the rhythm method and was given a string of beads of various colors to help her keep track of her ovulation. Several months later, she returned to one of the family planning centers, obviously pregnant. She told the sisters that she had hung the beads around a statue of Kali, and forgot about them. Then, she could not understand why she became pregnant.

As they had with her practices at Nirmal Hriday, detractors criticized Mother Teresa's stance on abortion and sterilization. Many argued that there were too many unwanted children in India and that there was no way that the Missionaries of Charity could possibly care for every single one. Although abortion clinics were available, they were rare and costly, hardly justifying Mother Teresa's outrage. Outlawing abortions might cause women to try to abort their unborn child themselves, often with terrible and fatal results. In the face of such criticism, Mother Teresa stood her ground and never veered away from the Church's teachings on birth control and abortion. But the controversy was far from over; in the years to come, Mother Teresa would be a visible target for pro-choice advocates the world over.

## REACHING OUT IN OTHER WAYS

Besides organizing the children's homes, Mother Teresa reached out to the poor in other ways. In 1956, she organized her first mobile clinic to help those who could not get to one of the free clinics. She was aided by Catholic Relief Services in New York City, which donated $5,000 to transform an old van into a traveling medical dispensary that visited the slums throughout the city offering free medical services. With the help of some doctors, a small laboratory was set up in Shishu Bhavan to do medical testing.

The Shishu Bhavan also became a buzzing center of activity for feeding the poor. In the home's small kitchen, the sisters cooked as much rice as they could, which they handed out along with bananas. On any given afternoon, there were anywhere from 50 to 100 women with children waiting to receive food. For many, this was the only meal of the day.

There were some hazards in providing the free food. On one occasion, the sisters had nothing to give out for that day, for the agency that supplied them had stopped sending food to the home. The hungry crowd grew angrier and angrier; some even tried to set fire to the home. At one point Mother Teresa pushed back with surprising strength a whole line of women who rushed forward to receive their food. It was only because of the arrival of the police and fire brigade that the incident did not escalate into something more serious. On another, less dangerous occasion, the kitchen ran out of plates and the sisters used dinner plates from the Motherhouse to give to the poor.

## TENDING TO THE UNCLEAN

Mother Teresa introduced the mobile dispensary in 1956 in response to another growing problem on the Calcutta streets: lepers. Earlier, the Gobra hospital, which housed many of the city's leprosy cases, had closed,

leaving thousands of patients with no place to go. Mother Teresa had lob-
bied hard against the closing, but growing pressure from local residents
and developers, who wanted the hospital moved away from the area,
forced the city to shut down the facility. A new hospital for lepers was
soon built further outside the city limits.

Mother Teresa, realizing that it would be difficult for the former patients of Gobra to go to the new facility, decided to open up her own
clinic. Like the former Gobra facility, she found a site that was centrally
located, which would make it easier for patients to receive treatment.
However, residents in the neighborhood, upon learning of the proposed
clinic, did their best to stop her efforts. On one occasion, when she arrived in the neighborhood to inspect the site, she was met by angry
neighborhood residents who began throwing stones at her. She took the
angry response in stride and remarked that it appeared that God did not
want the clinic in this area. She would pray for guidance.

As if in answer to her prayers, some American benefactors donated an
ambulance to the Missionaries of Charity. Mother Teresa hoped the vehicle would be the first of many mobile leprosy clinics. More help came from
a Dr. Sen, a physician and specialist in the treatment of skin disease and
leprosy. Sen had recently retired from the Carmichael Hospital for Tropi-
cal Diseases. Unsure of what to do with his free time and having heard of
the works of the Missionaries of Charity, he offered his services. Mother
Teresa gratefully accepted. Assisting Dr. Sen were three sisters who had
received nurse's training.

In September 1957, the first mobile leprosy clinic was launched. The
ambulance could hold six persons along with a generous supply of medicine, food, and medical records. Traveling from slum to slum, and also
making a stop outside the walls of the Loreto convent, the Missionaries of
Charity sought out the city's lepers. In time, eight treatment stations were
established throughout Calcutta offering hope to the city's 30,000 persons
afflicted by leprosy. The bright blue vehicle soon became a recognized
symbol of help and comfort. At each stop, the sisters handed out vitamins
and medicine, along with packets of food. By January 1958, over 600 lepers regularly sought treatment from the mobile clinic.

## A HIDEOUS DISEASE

In trying to help those afflicted by leprosy, Mother Teresa faced a special kind of problem. The disease, also known as Hansen's disease, has
been documented since biblical times. It is a particularly insidious ailment, striking people with little warning. The bacterium that causes lep-

rosy attacks the nervous system and destroys the body's ability to feel pain. Without pain, people injured themselves without always knowing it. Injuries become infected and resulted in tissue loss. Fingers and toes become shortened and deformed as the cartilage is absorbed into the body.

Early symptoms include discolored or light patches on the skin accompanied by loss of feeling. When the nerves are affected, small muscles become paralyzed, which leads to the curling of the fingers and thumb. When leprosy attacks nerves in the legs, there is no sensation in the feet. The feet can become subject to erosion through untended wounds and infection. If the facial nerves are affected, a person loses the blinking reflex of the eye, which can eventually lead to dryness, ulceration, and blindness. Bacilli entering the mucous lining of the nose can lead to internal damage and scarring, which in time causes the nose to collapse. The disease is assisted in its spread by unsanitary conditions, coughing, and sneezing. In a small household with poor sanitation, it is easy for the entire family to become infected.

The disease also carried with it, in India and elsewhere, a deep social stigma. The fear of becoming contaminated often prompts lepers to be banished. After the Gobra hospital closed, there was no place for many of the lepers in Calcutta to go except the slums and the countryside, where many died neglected. Even when a person recovered from the disease, they were still shunned by the community and often could not find housing, work, or help—the social stigma of the disease was that prevalent.

Although leprosy had all but disappeared in Europe and North America by the sixteenth century, it still existed in Asia, Africa, South America, and the Middle East. In 1873 Dr. Armauer Hansen of Norway discovered the bacteria that causes the disease, and a cure was almost a century away. During the 1950s, when Mother Teresa opened her first mobile clinics, leprosy was treated with dapsone pills. However, the leprosy bacilli began developing dapsone resistance hindering successful treatment.

## TITLAGARH

For those stricken with leprosy, there was one place outside of Calcutta to go—Titlagarh, an industrial suburb located about an hour's drive from Calcutta. Near the railway lines, a cluster of shanties had sprung up on either side. It was a village of the poor, with the lepers occupying the hovels alongside a swamp. The area was a human cesspool: there was no drainage or sewage, no drinking water, and no electricity. Even the wretchedly poor had nothing to do with the lepers. Townspeople and the police also stayed away for fear of infection. As a result, crime was rampant and indiscriminate; violence and murder were everyday happenings. The lepers, because of their disease and poverty, could not seek out treatment; no doctor, clinic, or hospital in Titlagarh would see them.

In the meantime, even with the success of the mobile clinic, Mother Teresa and her sisters realized that there were still a number of patients from Titlagarh who could not afford the bus or train fare every week to seek help. Those who could often found themselves banned from riding. In addition, Mother Teresa and the sisters were seeing more cases of newborns afflicted with leprosy; and it was a burden for mothers to come to the clinics. Many patients asked Mother Teresa to open a permanent clinic for them nearer to home.

When she made her first visit to Titlagarh, Mother Teresa realized that something needed to be done. Within a few months, she had established a small clinic in a shed near the railway lines. A few sisters were sent to handle the enormous caseload for the Titlagarh clinic. But it soon became evident that more needed to be done.

To draw attention to the plight of the lepers, Mother Teresa turned once again to her lay volunteers and benefactors. Many groups, hearing of the living conditions of the lepers, banded together to support a citywide collection to help them. The symbol used for the collection drive was a bell, the ancient symbol of the so-called unclean, but now pressed into service as a symbol of compassion. The slogan of the collection drive was Touch the Leper with Your Compassion; and the saying was carried on posters, signs, newspapers, and on the mobile van, too. The citywide campaign made it possible for even more lepers to be treated by uncovering other areas where groups of lepers resided.

Finally work was begun on the construction of a more permanent building. But that project ran into early difficulties. The first attempts to improve the living conditions of the railway site were met with opposition from gang leaders who ran most of the illegal activities in the area. Stones greeted the volunteers who were cleaning up the site, but they persisted. Construction of two small cottages at last began, and with them, resistance to the construction faded. The gang leaders fled and many of the residents pitched in to help with the building. In addition to the clinic, which opened in March 1959, the facility housed a rehabilitation center, a hospital, and a cafeteria. An assortment of utility buildings was added during a 10-year period. By the time construction was finished in 1968, the buildings constituted a mile-long stretch. Mother Teresa asked the municipality of Titlagarh for water, sewers, and electricity for the area. Children were put into local schools, and slowly small shops and stalls appeared in the area where once only crime and violence had flourished.

But no sooner had the clinic opened than the municipal leaders feared an influx of lepers would come to Titlagarh. They begged Mother Teresa to consider opening yet another facility for lepers. With that in mind, Mother Teresa turned to her next project: Shantinagar.

## SHANTINAGAR

In 1961, Mother Teresa received a gift from the Indian government: 34 acres of land located about 200 miles from Calcutta. She would pay the government an annual fee of one rupee a year for the land. The land was uncultivated, almost a jungle in appearance. With funds raised by German children singing at a charity concert, Mother Teresa began construction of Shantinagar—The Place of Peace for Lepers.

There was not enough money to complete the project. Hoping for a miracle, the Missionaries of Charity prayed for guidance. Their prayers were answered in 1965 in the form of a white 1964 Lincoln Continental automobile. The car was originally a present from American Catholics to Pope Paul VI. The pope had the car specially flown in for his state visit to India in 1964. While there, he visited Mother Teresa and the home at Nirmal Hriday and was so touched by the work of the Missionaries of Charity that he gave the car to Mother Teresa before he left. Having no practical use for the car, Mother Teresa raffled it off, raising a much larger sum of money than she would have by simple selling the automobile. In the end, the raffle netted the order of approximately 460,000 rupees or $100,000. With the funds raised by the raffle, Mother Teresa could pay for the main hospital block at Shantinagar.

In 1968, Mother Teresa sent Sister Francis Xavier along with several other sisters to Shantinagar to oversee the construction and maintenance of the grounds. Within the next two years, a number of key buildings went up including a rehabilitation center and cottage for lepers built by the patients themselves. In addition, flowering trees and shrubs, fruit trees, and vegetable gardens were planted on the grounds. The nearby pond was stocked with fish, all with an eye to promoting self-sufficiency among the residents.

In time, the home for lepers offered treatment and a chance at a normal life for almost 400 lepers and their families. New arrivals were taught to make bricks in order to construct new homes for future patients. The residents tended their own cattle, grew their own rice and wheat, and tilled their own gardens. Others ran a grocer's shop. Some residents made baskets, which are used in the nearby coal mines. There is even a printing press. Shantinagar also has its own local government with its leaders elected from among the residents. Medical treatment is not far away, and with the advent of better drugs since the 1970s, many lepers had a chance to recover from their illness. There is also a Shishu Bhavan on the premises, where children can live and be protected from the more infectious patients.

With each new success and each new undertaking, it was becoming clear that Mother Teresa possessed extraordinary vision. She was making a name for herself, not only throughout Calcutta, but in India and beyond. Her great determination to help those who could not help themselves had earned her a host of supporters and a growing number of critics. As the size and scale of the Missionaries of Charity grew, so did the seeds of controversy. By the end of the 1950s, it was clear that Mother Teresa and her order would no longer toil in anonymity.

## NOTES

1. Mother Teresa with Jaya Chaliha and Edward Le Joly, *The Joy in Loving: A Guide to Daily Living* (New York: Viking, 1996), p. 327.
2. Mother Teresa with Chaliha and Le Joly, *Joy,* p. 371.

# Chapter 8

# THE GROWTH OF A MIRACLE

By the late 1950s, Mother Teresa found herself becoming quite newsworthy, at least in Calcutta, where she was the subject of several articles in both the Indian and English newspapers. This attention marked the beginning of a remarkable relationship between Mother Teresa and the Indian press. For one thing, the articles about Mother Teresa and the Missionaries of Charity often resulted in donations to the order. Some of the gifts came in the form of money; others donated supplies and their time.

The wife of a British businessman and a former Loreto student, Aruna Paul, helped teach children in the slums. She also organized Christmas parties for the children. After her own children were born, she made a point of having birthday parties for the children in Shishu Bhavan on the same day as her own children's celebrations. She also made a point of taking her children with her to Shishu Bhavan to impress upon them how fortunate they were. Paul also had access to a textile factory; through her efforts, the sisters received new saris every year. Years later, Paul recalled that Mother Teresa, prior to her traveling, never seemed hurried and that she always had time for everyone who came to see her. But that would all soon change as Mother Teresa began capturing the attention of a much wider audience, while recognizing there were other places in the world that might benefit from her vision.

## SETTING FOOT ON THE WORLD STAGE

For nearly 10 years, the work done by the Missionaries of Charity had been confined to Calcutta. This was in agreement with church law, which prohibited new orders to open houses outside of the diocese. Initially, Mother Teresa realized that between the archbishop's emphatic enforcement of this rule, and the horrific problems she faced in Calcutta, expansion of any kind was clearly out of the question.

But, in 1959, things had changed. There was one year left before the probationary period of the Missionaries of Charity formally ended, and the sisters were eager to take their mission outside of Calcutta and begin work in other parts of India. When Mother Teresa went to Archbishop Périer, he relented. But he told Mother Teresa that her work could only expand into other areas of the country, not beyond. She agreed. New houses of the Missionaries of Charity were established—and warmly welcomed by church and city officials—in Delhi and Jhansi. The news of their work reached the highest echelons of Indian government; at the dedication of a children's home in Delhi, the Prime Minister of India, Jawaharlal Nehru, was in attendance. When introduced to him, Mother Teresa proceeded to tell the prime minister of her order. Gently stopping her, Nehru replied that he did not need to hear of her work; he knew all about it and that was why he had come to the ceremony. The Missionaries of Charity also sent a group of nuns to Ranchi, a city located in the extremely poor state of Bihar. Here, many girls from the local tribes were recruited to become Missionaries of Charity with great success.

In Bombay, a city with numerous Catholic churches and schools, the Missionaries of Charity were welcomed by none other than the head of the Roman Catholic Church in Bombay, Cardinal Valerian Gracias. After a short tour of the city, Mother Teresa angered many of the residents with her comment that the slums of Bombay were worse than those in Calcutta. But many others recognized that beside the many palatial homes found in the city were also tall buildings with little ventilation, no indoor plumbing, and very little fresh air. With Cardinal Gracias's blessing, Mother Teresa soon opened a home for the dying, similar to Nirmal Hriday.

In the autumn of 1960, Mother Teresa looked beyond the borders of her adopted country and accepted an invitation to speak at the National Council for Catholic Women to be held in Las Vegas, Nevada. Although it seemed an unlikely destination for a woman considered a saint throughout India, Mother Teresa went with the hope of raising more funds for the Missionaries of Charity.

By this time, Mother Teresa was 50 years old and in charge of 119 nuns, all but three of whom were Indian, and she wished to carry her message further. As it turned out, her reputation was already becoming established on the world stage. In the United States, she had appeared on the front page of an American magazine called *Jubilee: A Magazine for the Church and Her People* in 1958, which introduced her at least to the American Catholic community.

That October, Mother Teresa arrived in Los Angeles; from there she traveled to Las Vegas in the company of a former volunteer with the Missionaries of Charity, Katherine Bracken. Mother Teresa was to give a speech entitled "These Works of Love," in which she outlined the work of the Missionaries of Charity.

Mother Teresa had never spoken in public before; previously she had relied on others to do her talking for her. But speaking before 3,000 women, she discovered that what might have been a disadvantage actually was an advantage. Instead of a professional giving a polished speech, Mother Teresa showed herself to be a natural orator. She spoke easily of her life's work and that of the Missionaries of Charity in India. She stated she was not there to beg for donations; instead she continued to rely on God's providence for help. But she did remind her audience that they, too, could participate in doing something beautiful for God. As she was to discover, this approach proved far more effective in raising money than a direct appeal ever would. Afterwards, sitting in a booth in the convention hall, she watched as person after person stopped to put cash in a bag she carried with her. During the course of the day, the bag was emptied several times. Mother Teresa had discovered a powerful and successful way in which to raise funds for her projects. It was a formula from which she rarely deviated in the following years.

During her time in Las Vegas, Mother Teresa was less interested in the goings-on in the nearby casinos and nightclubs than she was to traveling in the desert. When asked what she thought of the city, she replied that the neon lights of the city's casinos and hotels reminded her of Dewali, the yearly Hindu festival of lights. As a souvenir of her visit to Nevada, she took some long cactus spines that she found in the desert. These were later twisted into a crown of thorns and placed on the head of the crucified Christ hanging behind the altar in the novitiate chapel of the Missionaries of Charity in Calcutta.

## A WHIRLWIND TOUR

From Las Vegas, Mother Teresa went to Peoria, Illinois, where she spoke to yet another group of Catholic women. Then it was on to Chicago and New York City. In each city, she was welcomed warmly and had little trouble in gathering more monies for the Missionaries of Charity. One disappointment in her itinerary came when a planned meeting with the

Democratic presidential candidate, John F. Kennedy, who was also Roman Catholic, did not take place. However, while in New York City, Mother Teresa met with Mother Anna Dengel, the Austrian-born founder of the Medical Mission Sisters, who had given Mother Teresa her early medical training in Patna a little more than a decade earlier. She also paid visits to Catholic Relief Services, and met with Bishop Fulton J. Sheen, who was a prominent radio and television personality in the United States. Sheen was the head of the American division of the foreign mission's organization, the Propagation of the Faith, which channeled donations to Catholic missions all over the world. But perhaps one of the most important contacts Mother Teresa made during this trip was with Marcolino Candau, director of the World Health Organization (WHO). She told Candau of her urgent need to provide for the lepers and their children in India. Candau told her that if she made her request through the Indian government, WHO would see that she received the necessary medical supplies.

From New York, Mother Teresa's next stop was London, where she spent one evening at the home of the sister of Indian Prime Minister Nehru, who encouraged her to expand her work, particularly where volunteers were concerned. Mother Teresa also met with a representative of the Oxfam aid agency and had her first television interview with a British journalist on the BBC.

Her next stop was Germany, where Mother Teresa enjoyed a greater reputation, having been featured in a news magazine *Weltelend* (*World Misery*), published by the German Catholic relief agency Miseror. The article had also shown photos of the terrible poverty in Calcutta as well as shots of Nirmal Hriday. Another news magazine *Erdkreis* (*Earth Circle*) had featured photos of Kalighat. As she stepped off the plane, wrapped in a rough wool blanket to protect her from the cold weather, Mother Teresa was greeted by a horde of German photographers and journalists.

In meeting with Miseror representatives, Mother Teresa outlined her plans for the construction of a new home for the dying in Delhi. She already had land set aside, but needed help in building the proposed facility. The organization, while generally preferring to fund self-help projects, readily agreed to her request. In return, they asked only that the Missionaries of Charity send financial statements to the organization to monitor how the money was spent. To their great surprise, Mother Teresa flatly rejected their request, stating that the sisters did not have time to spend on preparing complicated financial forms. She assured the officials that they should not worry about the money; each penny would go to the proposed project. But her refusal to keep detailed accounts marked the beginning of a practice that would continue and later become a source of much criticism. As Mother Teresa later argued, making out separate reports to each sponsor would be so time-consuming that the poor would suffer. Although she and her sisters recorded each donation with a letter, they did not keep detailed financial records of donations accepted and monies spent. As was her nature, Mother Teresa ignored complaints about the order's accounting practices.

Before leaving Germany, Mother Teresa also stopped to visit Dachau, one of the most infamous concentration camps in Nazi Germany, where more than 28,000 Jews died between 1933 and 1945. After listening to the history of the camp, Mother Teresa stated that the camp was to history what the Colosseum in Rome was to the Romans who threw the Christians to their death. In Mother Teresa's eyes, modern humans were behaving no better, and if anything, far worse.

After a brief visit to Switzerland, Mother Teresa stopped in Rome where she hoped to make a formal and personal plea to Pope John XXIII for the Missionaries of Charity to become a Society of Pontifical Right. If the pope agreed, it would mean that the Missionaries of Charity could begin working in other countries. However, when it came time to meet the pope, Mother Teresa, frightened at making the request directly to the pope, instead only asked for his blessing. She then made her request to Cardinal Gregory Agagianian, who agreed to take the matter under consideration. But it was clear that the Church recognized the value and importance of Mother Teresa not only to its missionary and humanitarian efforts, but to its efforts to spread the Gospel.

## A BRIEF REUNION

While in Rome, Mother Teresa arranged a reunion with her brother Lazar, whom she had not seen in more than 30 years. Lazar now lived in Palermo, Sicily, where he worked for a pharmaceutical firm. He was also married to an Italian woman and was the father of a 10-year-old daughter. During World War II, he had joined the Italian army after the Italian occupation of Albania. His defection to the Italian army earned him a death sentence in Albania; Lazar could never return to the land of his birth.

When the two met, they discussed the terrible predicament of Aga and their mother, who were still in Albania. The country, now a communist satellite of the Soviet Union, had made it virtually impossible for its residents to leave Albania. Mother Teresa had applied for a visa to visit the country, and possibly because of her brother, but more likely because of her own activities, she had been refused. Albania's atheist government did not look kindly on a religious figure, particularly one becoming internationally renowned.

And then all too soon, it was time to return home. Upon her arrival in Calcutta, Mother Teresa continued to work with her sisters, opening up new homes throughout India. For the next five years, new chapters appeared in cities and states throughout the country. Adopting the pattern established in Calcutta, the Missionaries of Charity assessed the needs of an area and adapted their programs. With each new house, each new school, each new mobile clinic, Mother Teresa's name and works gained greater and greater recognition. Still, it was not enough, and Mother Teresa waited anxiously for news from the Vatican.

## THE BIGGEST MIRACLE OF ALL

In February 1965, Mother Teresa finally received her answer: the Missionaries of Charity had received the pope's permission to become a Society of Pontifical Right. In his decree granting the right, Pope Paul VI, who had succeeded John XXIII, charged Mother Teresa and her order to continue carrying out their works of charity and to dedicate themselves to God. Now, Mother Teresa could carry her good works outside of India for the first time. In time, these works included clinics for those suffering from tuberculosis; antenatal clinics; clinics for general medical needs; mobile leprosy clinics; night shelters for the homeless; homes for children, the poor, and the dying; nursery schools, primary, and secondary schools; feeding programs; villages for lepers; commercial schools; vocational training in carpentry, metal work, embroidery and other skills; child-care and home-management classes; and aid in the event of emergencies and disasters such as floods, earthquakes, famine, epidemics, rioting and war.

Mother Teresa's first invitation came in 1965 when she was asked to open a house in Venezuela, to help many of the impoverished people who had lapsed in their Catholicism due to a lack of priests and nuns to sustain them. Archbishop James Robert Knox, the Internuncio to New Delhi, had already met with a South American bishop who impressed upon Knox the need for the Missionaries of Charity. Knox wanted Mother Teresa to accept the invitation and pressed her to do so. But Mother Teresa balked. She was not sure that her sisters were ready for such an undertaking. She wanted more time. Archbishop Knox told her that the needs of the Church were more important than the needs of her sisters. The matter was then settled. Mother Teresa and her order were going to Venezuela.

In July 1965, the Missionaries of Charity opened their first home outside India in Cocorote, Venezuela. Mother Teresa, accompanied by five sisters, came to the small town. Working in Cocorote also presented the Missionaries of Charity with a very different situation. Not only were they dealing with a different language, but also with a different culture. While in Cocorote, the sisters, for the first time, began cooperating in religious education. Because priests were in such short supply, the sisters took on the duties of preparing children to receive their First Communion and Confirmation, which were important Catholic rituals for children between the ages of 8 and 12.

By 1970, the duties of the sisters had expanded even more. After opening a house in Caracas, they received permission for three of their nuns to administer Holy Communion, a duty previously reserved for priests. This relaxing of rules allowed the Missionaries of Charity to offer Holy Communion to the sick and the dying. In addition, the sisters were busy conducting funerals, washing and cleaning for the elderly, and feeding the hungry. In 1972, the Missionaries of Charity helped with roof repairs when strong winds damaged several homes, leaving many without adequate shelter. In return for their many labors, the nuns might be rewarded with something simple: an egg from someone's hen, or a banana. The sisters accepted the gifts with gratitude.

## AN APPEAL FROM ROME

In 1968, Mother Teresa received another invitation, this time to work among the poor in Rome. The invitation came as a bit of a surprise. Rome already had more than 22,000 nuns belonging to 1,200 separate religious orders. Why, Mother Teresa thought, would the Church need yet another group to work with the poor? But this invitation was different; it came from none other than Paul VI himself.

Three years earlier, in July 1965, Mother Teresa was among a group of 40 persons granted an audience with the pope. Although Mother Teresa was overwhelmed at meeting the pope, as were the six other Missionaries of Charity who accompanied her, it appears Paul VI was taken with her. Asking for her prayers, he told Mother Teresa to write to him. Now, the pope was asking her directly for her help in working with Rome's poor.

That August, Mother Teresa and a handful of her nuns arrived in Rome to begin work. The area in which they were to work, known as the *borgate*, is located on the outskirts of Rome. Here live the city's poorest residents, many of whom could not even begin to pay the city's high rents. The area was home to thousands of immigrants from Sicily and Sardinia.

Rome's slums were also known for their distinctive architecture. Shelters known as *barraca,* a kind of barracks-like structure, sprawled for acres in the city's slums. The homes were also distinguished by their bright orange terra-cotta roofs, which were secured by heavy stones. Many of these homes lacked electricity, water, and sewage, though some enterprising souls were able to tap into the city's electrical power source to light their homes. Some families also planted small gardens near their homes, which, in addition to supplementing their diets, alleviated the barren and harsh landscape of poverty with a wondrous riot of color.

Initial attempts to find a house for the order were futile; there appeared to be nothing for them. Finally, Mother Teresa found a *barracche.* It was by far the poorest and shabbiest residence that the sisters had resided in, something that appealed to Mother Teresa a great deal. With the exception of the house being wired for electricity, the residence was from all appearances no different from the others. There was no plumbing; the nuns would have to make do with the nearby fountain from which residents drew their water. In time, the Missionaries of Charity instituted many of the same programs for the poor of Rome that they provided elsewhere.

## A GROWING MISSION

Over the next several years, Mother Teresa and her Missionaries of Charity continued to open new homes around the world. In 1967, the order opened its first home in Sri Lanka. In September 1968, a month after traveling to Rome, Mother Teresa journeyed to Tabora, Tanzania, where the sisters opened their first mission in Africa. A year later, the Missionaries of Charity were in Australia, where they opened up a center for the Aborigines. From this point on and well into the next decade, a new mission center opened somewhere in the world approximately every six months.

The Missionaries of Charity were growing in other ways, too. By 1963, Mother Teresa realized that men were better suited for certain kinds of work, such as working with young boys, than her nuns were. After consulting with Father Van Exem, she petitioned the archbishop of Calcutta for his permission to create a new branch of the order: the Missionary Brothers of Charity. The archbishop did not have to think very long; almost immediately he agreed to the request.

But there were issues to settle before the new order could get underway. Men were reluctant to join because the order was still unrecognized. To become recognized meant that the order needed to grow and have the proper leadership to provide guidance and direction. Even though the brothers were aligned with the Missionaries of Charity, under Church law Mother Teresa could not head a male congregation. She tried to engage the services of two other priests, but for a number of reasons could not convince either man to leave his order to take charge of the new congregation. Finally, a young priest applied for the position; Mother Teresa, even though she did not know him personally, agreed to have him take on the responsibility of directing the new order.

In 1966, an Australian Jesuit, Father Ian Travers-Ball, became the head of the Missionary Brothers, changing his name to Brother Andrew. Travers-Ball was a young and charismatic presence within the order. He was familiar with conditions in India having come to the country in 1954 as a new priest. He was interested in working with the poor, and specifically with Mother Teresa and the Missionaries of Charity.

Early on, Brother Andrew believed it was necessary for the Brothers of Charity to establish their own presence and identity. Although he admired Mother Teresa, Travers-Ball also wished to escape her domination. To establish a base for the Brothers, Brother Andrew rented a small house in Kidderpore, which Mother Teresa purchased. Along with a dozen young homeless boys, Brother Andrew moved into the home. In time, the house settled into a routine that was far different from the goings-on at Motherhouse.

In general, the Brothers adopted a style of working with the poor that was far less regimented. They were less sheltered than the Sisters, which allowed them access to the poor community in ways that the Sisters did not enjoy. The more informal approach enabled the Brothers to be more adaptable to cultural and regional differences than the Sisters. And because their focus was on helping poor boys, their homes tended to be smaller and more close-knit.

One of the first places the Brothers began work was at the Howrah railway station where many young poor boys lived. Much as Mother Teresa did when she began working among the poor, the Brothers started out by establishing contact and helping the boys in small ways, such as passing out bars of soap or helping get medical treatment for those in need. Gradually, the Brothers organized an evening meal for the boys at the station. Some boys were taken in and given refuge where they could receive vocational training. Along with boys residing at the Shishu Bhavan, several were then transferred to other houses in and around the city, such as Nabo Jeevan (New Life), or Dum-Dum where there was a radio-repair workshop. Boys suffering from medical or mental handicaps were taken to Nurpur, a farm located about 20 miles outside of Calcutta, where they learned to farm. The Brothers also became heavily involved with mobile leprosy clinics and, in time, would take over the day-to-day work at the leprosy colony in Titlagarh.

Like Mother Teresa's own Missionaries of Charity, the Brothers grew rapidly. Within a decade of their creation, Brother Andrew opened up the first overseas house in war-torn Vietnam. From there, the order began opening houses all over the world, usually in places where the Missionaries of Charity did not have a presence. In 1975, the Brothers opened a house in a poor, crime-infested neighborhood in Los Angeles, California, where they began working with drug addicts and alcoholics who had been living on the street.

There was no shortage of rough neighborhoods in the world, and Brother Andrew sought out as many as he could find, establishing homes in Hong Kong, Japan, Taiwan, Korea, Guatemala, the Philippines, El Salvador, the Dominican Republic, Haiti, and Brazil. Everywhere they went, the Brothers undertook the jobs they knew best. Their mission, more than that of the Missionaries of Charity, brought them into contact with the residents of many a city's mean streets and society's outcasts: the criminals, the drug addicts, and the hopeless alcoholics. The Brothers also continued their work with orphaned and wayward boys. Wherever they went, they established soup kitchens and helped those in need to receive medical attention.

Still, the Brothers' road to success was not without its bumps. Predictably, Brother Andrew and Mother Teresa clashed over the order's management. One issue was dress; Brother Andrew requested that the brothers wear no uniform and instead dress in jeans and T-shirts. While this made them more accessible, it also made them at times harder to distinguish, and on more than one occasion, a brother was picked up along with those he was helping to spend a night at the city jail. Mother Teresa wished for the Brothers to wear their clerical garb. She also did not agree with Brother Andrew's willingness to delegate authority and wished for tighter, stricter management, much as she did with her own order. The final straw came when Mother Teresa established a contemplative branch of the Brothers without consulting Brother Andrew. Her actions caused a temporary rift between the two orders; in 1987, Brother Andrew left the order. His replacement, Brother Geoff, brought with him a management style and an attitude that was more complementary to Mother Teresa's vision for the Missionaries of Charity Brothers.

## COME AND SEES AND CO-WORKERS

Assisting the Missionaries of Charity and the Brothers were volunteers whom Brother Andrew called Come and Sees. This group consisted mainly of young people interested in working with the Brothers for a few weeks or months. Some were interested in joining the order, but wanted to see if they were capable of handling the work. Mother Teresa had adopted a similar practice with her own missions for young women who might be interested in joining her order.

Also assisting Mother Teresa and her Missionaries of Charity were hundreds of volunteers, called Co-Workers. The term was borrowed from Mahatma Ghandi, who referred to his helpers by the same name. Like Ghandi, Mother Teresa's Co-Workers were men, women, and children from all over the world. They came from a variety of backgrounds and represented a number of different religions. All shared an interest in helping the poor.

Among the first Co-Workers helping Mother Teresa were the Gomes family, and the many doctors, nurses, and dentists who donated free medical services. By the 1950s, a more formal organization of Co-Workers had been established, largely through the efforts of British wives who were involved with various social services in Calcutta. When a number of these women returned to England, they began meeting, and by 1960, a Mother Teresa committee was formed that began working with the poor in English cities. By the 1990s, approximately 30,000 Co-Workers were volunteering in the United Kingdom.

Smaller groups of Co-Workers appeared in other countries as well. In the United States, there are approximately 10,000. In Europe, the numbers are much smaller, with only a few hundred active volunteers. Still, the rise of one group has often led to the formation of another. Although forbidden to engage in fund-raising or publicity, the group publishes *Co-Workers Newsletter,* which goes out to all members. There is no paid office or staff to put out the newsletter; all work is donated. Further, Mother Teresa stipulated that all collection centers for clothing or food are to be in someone's residence; there is to be no rental of a unit or storefront.

In some areas, Co-Workers handled donations of money which were turned over to the Missionaries or were spent to buy bulk purchases of necessities such as food, clothing, and medical supplies. The size of some of these donations are staggering even by today's standards: for instance, in 1990, 17,000,000 Belgian francs ($680,000 in 2004 dollars) were used to purchase powdered milk, while 200,000 Dutch guilders ($146,000 in 2004 dollars) bought protein biscuits. Both purchases were then sent to Missionaries of Charity houses in Africa, South and Central America, and Asia. An additional 3,000,000 Belgian francs ($120,000 in 2004 dollars) was spent to buy clothes bought at one-tenth of retail value and sent to various countries in Africa. Finally, 24 large containers of used clothing, blankets, and bandages that were collected door-to-door by British Co-Workers were sent to several countries in Asia.

But Mother Teresa emphasized to her volunteers not to wander away from more humbling tasks, whether it was writing a letter, washing clothes, or reading to the ill.

There is also a very special branch of the Co-Workers that was created during the 1960s: the Sick and Suffering Co-Workers. These are individuals who are old, infirm, or handicapped; they cannot help with the more strenuous activities of the other Co-Workers. This group offers prayers for Mother Teresa and the Missionaries of Charity's efforts. Quite often, these volunteers are linked with a member of the active Co-Workers in their area. Currently there are about 5,000 Sick and Suffering Co-Workers representing 57 countries.

## THE MEETING POINT

In 1968, Oliver Hunkin, head of religious programming for the BBC, called upon noted British journalist Malcolm Muggeridge, to ask whether he would do a short television interview with a relatively unknown nun from India. Hunkin's choice of Muggeridge was inspired. Muggeridge was well known for his agnosticism and mocking attitude toward organized religions. Having briefly entertained thoughts of becoming a priest at a young age, Muggeridge instead chose journalism as a career. However, he never completely let go of his deep Christian feelings, and much later in life returned to the Church. But for now, Muggeridge was a bit put out at the thought of conducting this interview, particularly since Hunkin had not given him much notice in order for him to prepare.

Muggeridge had never heard of Mother Teresa, but the next afternoon he found himself making his way to the Holy Child Convent in London to do the interview. Mother Teresa, looking visibly nervous, answered Muggeridge's questions in a small, halting voice. Gently, he led her through the story of her mission and what she hoped to accomplish, and avoided controversial questions completely; nor was there any appeal for donations on her part. At one point, Muggeridge feared that he would not be able to keep the interview going for the full 30 minutes. When the completed interview was broadcast for BBC executives, there was even some question about whether the lackluster and ordinary exchange should be televised.

But in the end, the interview aired in May 1968 on the BBC Sunday-night series, *Meeting Point*. The response was as unexpected as it was spectacular. So many British viewers were moved by the story of Mother

Teresa and the Missionaries of Charity, that within 10 days of the broadcast, £9,000 ($16,000 in 2004 dollars) were donated to the organization. Another story credits the interview with raising £25,000 (approximately $45,000 in 2004 dollars). Although the actual figure is in dispute, one thing is not: Mother Teresa struck a chord with the public. BBC officials were so taken aback by the response to the interview that they broadcast it again with even more donations coming in for the Missionaries of Charity.

## AN ACTUAL MIRACLE?

What, on the surface, appeared to have been a run-of-the-mill interview had a very profound effect on Malcolm Muggeridge. Later, he admitted that when he first saw Mother Teresa walk into the room, she appeared unique and significant. He was also very excited about the possibility of working with her again and asked the BBC to send him to Calcutta where he could film Mother Teresa in action.

In the spring of 1969, Muggeridge, accompanied by a cameraman and producer, left for Calcutta. Although initially reluctant to agree to the request, Mother Teresa eventually relented and gave the film crew her full cooperation. For the next five days, Muggeridge and his team followed Mother Teresa as she went about her daily routine. But it was the filming at Nirmal Hriday in which Muggeridge later claimed to have witnessed a photographic miracle.

Initially, both Muggeridge and Kenneth Macmillan, the cameraman, were reluctant to shoot inside the home because of the dimly lit interior. As it was, Macmillan had only a small light with him, and to get adequate light seemed an impossible task. However, he had recently purchased some new Kodak film, which he had not tried yet. He decided to go ahead and shoot footage inside Nirmal Hriday using the new film. When Muggeridge and his team returned to London, they began work on the documentary. Several weeks later, as they were reviewing rushes, or the unedited film footage, they watched for the first time the sequence shot at Nirmal Hriday. Macmillan recounted what happened next:

> It was surprising. You could see every detail. And I said: "That's amazing, that's extraordinary." And I was going to say…three cheers for Kodak. I didn't get a chance to say that though because Malcolm, sitting in the front row, spun round and said: "It's divine light! It's Mother Teresa. You'll find that it's divine light old boy."[1]

Macmillan also found himself besieged over the next several days by newspaper reporters asking him about the miracle he had witnessed.

The completed documentary *Something Beautiful for God* was shown for the first time in December 1969. It was a resounding success. Later, Muggeridge, Macmillan, and Peter Chafer, the producer, credited Mother Teresa for the film's reception, citing her as an extremely charismatic presence. However, both Chafer and Macmillan were reluctant to attribute the extraordinary lighting sequence at Nirmal Hriday to Divine Providence, even though when Macmillan used the film again in a low-light situation he got poor results.

The documentary not only boosted Mother Teresa's image worldwide, it also had an impact on the Missionaries of Charity. As a result of the film, there was a visible increase in the numbers of young women wishing to join the order. In 1970, a year after the documentary aired, 139 new candidates were received by the Missionaries of Charity. The new arrivals came from all over: Pakistan, Ceylon, Nepal, Malaysia, Yugoslavia, Germany, Malta, France, Mauritania, Ireland, Venezuela, Italy, and India. The total of the entire congregation stood at 585, of which 332 were fully professed nuns, 175 novices, and 78 postulants, a remarkable achievement for an order barely two decades old.

## NOTE

1. Anne Sebba, *Mother Teresa: Beyond the Image* (New York: Doubleday, 1997), p. 83.

# Chapter 9

# BLESSINGS AND BLAME

Thanks to the amazing success of the documentary *Something Beautiful for God*, Mother Teresa no longer just belonged to Calcutta or to India. She belonged to the world. Malcolm Muggeridge, the journalist who now emerged as one of Mother Teresa's most vocal and supportive champions, went on to write a book published under the same title in 1971. Using the transcript from the film as the basis of the text and incorporating many black and white photographs, the book illustrated Mother Teresa's work and life. Muggeridge also included nine pages of Mother Teresa's sayings, stating that, since Mother Teresa would never write about herself or her work, there should be a record of her own words.

The book enjoyed phenomenal success. It has rarely gone out of print, and over 30 years, has sold more than 300,000 copies. It has been reprinted 20 times and has been translated into 13 languages. Upon his death in 1990, Muggeridge donated the royalties from the book to Mother Teresa, the sum of which is about £60,000.

Between the film, the book, and Mother Teresa's own globe-trotting, both she and her order were very much in the public eye. Although that visibility was beneficial, particularly as Mother Teresa was trying to raise funds and awareness of the world's poor, it also left her vulnerable to growing dissent, criticism, and accusations. Despite Muggeridge's predictions that Mother Teresa would one day be awarded the Nobel Peace Prize, her application for the coveted award was rejected three times.

## NEW ADVENTURES

During the 1970s Mother Teresa continued her travels, both speaking and opening new homes for the Missionaries of Charity. The decade opened with a home established in Amman, Jordan. In December 1970, a novitiate, or center to train newcomers, opened in England; homes for the Missionaries opened in London's Paddington District and the Bronx, New York City in 1971. Mother Teresa and her Missionaries did not shy away from the world's troubled spots: in 1972, a new foundation opened in Belfast, Northern Ireland; in 1973, Mother Teresa opened another foundation working with the 380,000 Arab refugees who lived and worked in the Israeli-occupied Gaza strip. And so it continued throughout the decade with the high point coming in 1979 when the Missionaries of Charity opened 14 new foundations. As her missions spread across the world, Mother Teresa enjoyed the support of many world leaders. In the United States alone, she counted among her champions the wealthy Democratic Kennedy family and former Republican president Richard M. Nixon.

She also began receiving a number of honors. Her first came in 1962 when she was awarded the Magsaysay Award for International Understanding. That same year she received the Padma Shri, known as the Magnificent Lotus, India's second highest award. First, after hearing the news that she won, Mother Teresa would not accept it. However, after receiving permission, she traveled to New Delhi to accept the award from the president of India at that time, Dr. Rajendra Prasad.

In many cases, the awards came with substantial cash prizes. For instance, the money received from the Magsaysay award was used to purchase a home for children. In January 1971, Mother Teresa traveled to Rome where she accepted a check from Pope Paul VI for £10,000 (appx. $17,000) after being awarded the first Pope John XXIII Peace Prize. That money was directed toward the building of a leper colony on land donated by the Indian government. In 1971, she again traveled to New Delhi to accept from the Indian government the Nehru Award for International Understanding. In 1973, Mother Teresa became the first recipient of the Templeton Prize for Progress in Religion. She was chosen out of a field of 2,000 nominations by a panel of judges representing the world's major religions including Christianity, Islam, Judaism, Buddhism, and Hinduism. In every case, Mother Teresa graciously accepted each award in the name of the world's poor.

## BATTLING SPIRITUAL POVERTY

Mother Teresa was most familiar with the conditions of the poor in Third-World countries; however, when confronted with the poverty in Western countries, she was not only shocked but appalled. On more than one occasion, she noted with some irony how people in the West sent donations to her to help the poor in India, when at the same time they turned their backs on those in their own countries who were suffering and forgotten. In many areas, the Missionaries of Charity opened up Homes of Compassion for the destitute men and women living on the streets. The nuns also made a point of checking on the elderly and lonely who had no one to look after them.

For Mother Teresa, the poverty that confronted her in such societies as the United States and Great Britain was more a poverty of the spirit. It came in the form of loneliness and being unwanted, plaguing the homeless, the drifters, the alcoholics, and the mentally ill left to fend for themselves. What Mother Teresa found so troubling, as she traveled through the rough neighborhoods of London or New York City, was society's response to these people: shunning them, abandoning them, or leaving them at the mercy of those who were stronger.

Yet, Mother Teresa did not pass judgment on those societies. Instead, she tried to point out as gently as she could that God did not make the poor people in the world, nor did he create poverty and disorder. Rather, it was because people did not share enough with one another that some had plenty and others went without. When faced with the criticism that helping all the needy in the world was a never-ending and hopeless task, she replied that she and her sisters used themselves to save whom they could, when they could. If pressed hard to reason out her mission as a result of that first foray into the Calcutta slums over 20 years before, she might have been astounded to learn that she and her order had saved tens of thousands of lives. But numbers were meaningless to Mother Teresa; for her, each small act, each kindness extended toward those in need, was done in the name of Christ. That was all.

## LEADING BY EXAMPLE

As the number of foundations grew, Mother Teresa's schedule became more hectic. Because she kept close watch on the order, leading by example, it was important that she visit every motherhouse she could to check on the day-to-day goings on. For instance, she believed that the sisters must not waste any donations because others had sacrificed in order that they have them. Medicine and food were to be distributed as soon as possible to prevent spoilage. She asked that the priests who assisted in the spiritual welfare of the sisters not interfere in the internal affairs of the houses, particularly when it came to observing their vows of poverty. At no time should a congregation raise its standard of living; this meant going without simple things such as curtains for the motherhouse or bedspreads, which were invariably given away. Donations of washing ma-chines, carpets, or other creature comforts were also given away. As Mother Teresa continually reminded her sisters, the poor did without and so must they.

She wrote to each house as often as possible offering advice, wisdom, and comfort to her growing number of sisters. She wrote to parents thank-ing them for their daughters who had given their lives in service to God. She reminded her nuns to be cheerful and smile, as God needed and loved those who gave of themselves cheerfully. A cheerful disposition also at-tracted those who might be seeking a vocation with the Missionaries of Charity. She shared news of her travels, her visits with dignitaries, and hu-morous incidents that had occurred.

Even as she was becoming more well known, Mother Teresa remained as unobtrusive as possible. She commonly slept in the luggage racks of third-class train compartments or shared a seat on a train or a bus between the wife of a farmer and some livestock. On those occasions when she had a seat to herself, she made the most of it, using the time for reflection, often writing small notes or letters to her sisters and benefactors.

Yet, she declined the offers of regular income that were beginning to arise more frequently. She emphasized repeatedly that fund-raising was not her work, fearing that the Missionaries of Charity would become a business rather than a labor of love. She squarely placed her life and that of her congregations in God's hands, fully trusting that Providence would provide for her needs in helping the poor. Her rejections of some dona-tions were on the face of it astounding, yet completely in character. Once she rejected an offer from New York City's Cardinal Terence Cooke, which would provide $500 a month for each Sister working in Harlem, asking him if he believed that God was going to be bankrupt in New York City.

## LOSS AND FAILINGS

The 1970s were an extraordinary period of growth for the Missionaries of Charity and of growing recognition for Mother Teresa. Still, the decade was not without its low points as Mother Teresa suffered both personal losses and public failures. She may also have come to realize that not all things were possible through faith and love alone.

The year 1970 began with a troubling letter from her sister Aga, who was living with their mother in Tirana, Albania. Drana was in ill health and her condition was worsening. On top of that, life under communist rule was extremely difficult and the two were having a hard time making ends meet. For Mother Teresa, this was a bitter blow; her divine Providence, which had made possible the impossible, seemed strangely absent now. But she took the news with a strong heart, yet sad that there was nothing she could do to help her mother and sister when she had found ways to help so many others around the world.

Yet, June 1970, Mother Teresa had a bittersweet homecoming. The Red Cross extended an invitation to her to visit Yugoslavia. From there she made the journey to Prizren, where her family originated, and then traveled to Skopje, the city of her birth. Here she met with the local bishop and visited the shrine at Letnice, where she had often visited to pray and meditate as a young girl. She made it known that she hoped one day to return to Skopje to open a Missionary of Charity home.

Later that year, Drana wrote to her son Lazar stating that her only wish was to see him, his family, and her daughter Gonxha before she died. Both Lazar and Mother Teresa worked hard to bring Aga and Drana to Italy for a reunion. At one point, Mother Teresa, while on a visit to Rome, paid a visit to the Albanian embassy seeking permission to bring her mother and sister to Italy. Lazar, though limited in what he could do, tried working with Catholic Relief Services to help relocate Aga and Drana in the event that they would be allowed to leave. These attempts proved futile: the Albanian government refused to permit either Aga or Drana to leave the country.

Mother Teresa then thought about traveling to Albania. But, to her dismay, she learned that while she might be allowed to enter the country, communist authorities could very well prevent her from leaving. Finally, on July 12, 1972, Mother Teresa received word that her mother had died. Not more than a year later, on August 25, 1973, more sad news came, when she learned that her sister Aga had also died. Mother Teresa's pain and grief were not so much for herself, but for the mother and sister who suffered.

The Missionaries of Charity also suffered severe setbacks during the 1970s. In 1971, after much fanfare, the order opened a house in Belfast, Northern Ireland, in the Catholic ghetto of Ballymurphy. Belfast was, at the time, a city under siege, as Catholic and Protestant factions engaged in almost daily violence. Mother Teresa sent four sisters who came with a violin and two blankets each. The house where they were to live had been previously occupied by a priest who had been shot just as he had finished administering last rites to a wounded man. The house was completely empty and had been the target of vandals. Undaunted, the sisters began working with a small group of Anglican nuns in the hope of helping to end strife in the city.

After only 18 months in Belfast, the sisters left, stating that they were unwanted and saw no need to risk further danger to themselves. Mother Teresa preferred to see their leaving, however, not as a failure, but as a call, for the sisters were obviously needed somewhere else. She sent them to Ethiopia where they were to help victims of a terrible drought that ravaged the country.

During the 1980s, the Missionaries of Charity experienced more bad luck, when in March 1980 someone set a fire at a home for destitute women run by the order in Kilburn, London. Ten residents of the shelter and one volunteer died in the blaze. The arsonist was never found. In 1986, two sisters were drowned in Dehra Dun, India, when a wooden bridge collapsed during a heavy rain, sending their ambulance into the river below. Although Mother Teresa offered prayers for the dead, no doubt both incidents weighed heavily upon her.

Even more painful for Mother Teresa was the number of professed sisters choosing to leave the Missionaries of Charity. Of the original 12 women who became the order's first nuns, two eventually left, as well as a small number of others over the years. Their reasons for leaving were many: some chose to serve God in another way, others wished to leave because of ill health. Some even fell in love and wished to marry and raise families. Mother Teresa did not resent the women's choices; in fact she often thanked them for their time and effort in their service to the order. Still, it clearly saddened her to lose members.

Despite these setbacks, the Missionaries of Charity continued to grow. By 1979, there were 158 foundations established throughout the world. There were 1,187 professed sisters, 411 novices, and 120 postulants. What was perhaps most amazing about the continued growth of the order was that it came at a time when religious vocations for the Church were generally on the decline. It appeared that the total commitment to a life of poverty and the complete surrender of the self in the service of God held tremendous appeal for women everywhere. For Mother Teresa, the continued arrival of newcomers ready to work for the poor was heartwarming. Each week it seemed a new group left Motherhouse bound for some destination where they were needed. As Mother Teresa once remarked, "If there are poor on the moon, we shall go there too."[1]

## THE FIRST VOLLEY

One of the first and fiercest attacks on Mother Teresa's work came during a crisis in the newly formed country of Bangladesh. Between 1947 and 1971, before gaining its independence, Bangladesh formed the eastern part of Pakistan and was called East Pakistan. Before the partition of India into independent India and Pakistan in 1947, the area that now forms Bangladesh, or the "land of Bengal," had been the eastern part of the Bengal province.

In December 1971 fighting broke out on the Indo-Pakistan border in the west. The Indian army also invaded East Pakistan and in two weeks had control of the country. The Bangladesh government-in-exile established itself in Dhaka on December 22, 1971, but in January 1972, the leaders returned to the country to begin governing the new nation.

But independence for Bangladesh came at a high price. In the nine months of fighting, three million Bengalis had died and over one million homes had been destroyed. Many of the people killed were professionals—teachers, doctors, lawyers, skilled workers, and engineers. Tea plantations and many jute mills were damaged. Added to this vast physical destruction, including the great damage to the transportation system, was the social disruption of the country. Many of the ten million refugees returned to find their homes in ruins. Some sought shelter in the nearest sewer pipe.

In addition, the country suffered great internal strife. Though much of the destruction had been the direct result of actions taken by the Pakistani army, many non-Bengalis in East Pakistan, the Biharis, had played a role as a paramilitary force, working with the Pakistani army against the Bengalis. After the war, many of the Biharis were placed in camps, and some were killed. The atrocities did not end there. Pakistani troops reportedly raped 4,000 women, though some place the number as high as 200,000.

On January 14, 1972, Mother Teresa announced that she was going to Bangladesh with 10 of her nuns to assist the rape victims, many of whom were now in the advanced stages of pregnancy. Traveling to Khulna, Pabna, Rajshahi, and Dhaka, Mother Teresa and her nuns sought out these women, in the hope of arranging adoptions for as many as possible. Because rape is a very serious crime in Islam, the victim is often ostracized by her family, friends, and perhaps even an entire village. For many women, giving up any children who might have been conceived as a result of the rape was the only option.

In Dhaka, the nuns were given the use of an old convent as a home for the women. But there were few who came seeking help. Some victims did not conceive, while others tried to terminate their pregnancies themselves. Eventually, the convent was turned into another Shishu Bhavan for orphaned and abandoned children.

As altruistic as Mother Teresa's motives may have been, there was at least one person who did not view her actions in Bangladesh in the same light. Australian feminist and writer Germaine Greer, a Roman Catholic, reported in an article written for the magazine the *Independent* in 1990, another purpose behind Mother Teresa's humanitarian mission:

> When she went to Dacca two days after its liberation from the Pakistanis in 1972, 3,000 naked women had been found in the army bunkers. Their saris had been taken away so that they would not hang themselves. The pregnant ones needed abortions. Mother Teresa offered them no option but to bear the offspring of hate. There is no room in Mother Teresa's universe for the moral priorities of others. There is no question of offering suffering women a choice.[2]

But Greer wasn't done yet. She went on to write that, according to lay workers with whom she had spoken at the time, pregnant women suffering from complications attributed to both physical abuses and malnutrition—as well as women who had miscarried—were turned away from Mother Teresa's clinics. According to Greer, the women had been accused by the Missionaries of Charity working at the clinics of trying to abort their unborn children. Further, when the new Bengali government banned the export of Bengali orphans, Mother Teresa, through some means, was allowed to place Bengali babies with Catholic families abroad. And, according to Greer's sources, no one at the Family Planning Association who knew of the incidents was allowed to say anything critical of Mother Teresa or her actions.

## THE NOBEL PEACE PRIZE

By the 1970s, Mother Teresa had emerged as a powerful human-interest story for newspapers and magazines around the world. This tiny nun, barely over five feet tall, had a number of powerful leaders and politicians as her friends. In spite of the growing number of financial donations made to the Missionaries of Charity, Mother Teresa refused to allow herself any indulgences that would interfere with her vow of poverty. And, though small in stature, she clearly wielded considerable power.

One of the more interesting stories that was done on her during this period came from *Time* magazine. In December 1975, the magazine not only devoted a long article to her, but also chose her for the cover of the magazine. Mother Teresa explained that she only agreed to sit for the photographer after having prayed at mass that morning. She asked God, that for every picture the photographer took, one soul be released from purgatory.

The article "Saints among Us," besides providing an overview of Mother Teresa's work, also suggested that many supporters considered her a living saint, a title Mother Teresa herself rejected. The article also discussed the qualities that made a saint. For instance, many saints lived their lives outside of conventional society and were often considered misfits. People, then, who tended to conform to cultural norms rarely went on to exhibit saintly qualities. As one theology professor noted, saints tend to be on the outer edge along with the maniacs, geniuses, and idiots. Saints also broke the rules of society in order to carry out their work.

The *Time* magazine article highlighted not only Mother Teresa's saintly qualities, but also her shrewd sense of organization and her great compassion for the poor. However, the article also went on to point out that there were a number of individuals who had also devoted their lives to the poor, but who were not as well known as Mother Teresa. These included Dorothy Day, founder of the Catholic Worker Movement; the Norwegian medical missionary Annie Skau, who lived and worked in Hong Kong; Dr. Cicely Saunders, founder of the Hospice movement; and the Coptic monk Matta el Meskin, also known as Matthew the Poor.

By this time, Mother Teresa had received numerous accolades and awards. Still, there were many who believed that she was overlooked and wished her to receive what they considered to be the most important and prestigious award in the world: the Nobel Peace Prize.

Those who select nominees for the Nobel Peace Prize may be from one of seven categories, including members of the International Court of Arbitration in The Hague; active and former members of the Nobel Committee of the Norwegian Parliament; advisors appointed by the Norwegian Nobel Institute; university professors of political science, law, history, and philosophy; and lastly, those who have won the prize themselves.

Mother Teresa had first been nominated for the prize in 1972, but no prize was awarded that year. Many of her supporters, among them Malcolm Muggeridge, again put her name in nomination in 1975. This time her nomination was supported by a number of important and influential individuals including Senator Edward Kennedy; Robert McNamara, then head of the World Bank; the National Council of Catholic Women; the Mayor of Addis Ababa; the head of the UN Disaster Relief Organization, Faruk Berkol; and a number of nuns in Spain.

But the prize eluded her again and went instead to Andrei Sakharov, the noted Russian scientist and human rights advocate. In 1977, Mother Teresa's name was put forth yet another time. Again the Nobel committee passed her over for the award, which was instead given to the organi-

zation Amnesty International for championing human rights around the
world. She later joked that the prize would only come to her when Jesus
thought it was time.

Then, in 1979, her name was put forward again, only with much less
fanfare. Although the name of the person who put forward Mother
Teresa's name has never been publicly acknowledged, it is thought to have
been Robert McNamara. McNamara had known Mother Teresa for almost two decades and was very familiar with her work with the poor. He
had also worked with her on occasion in the Food for Peace program. In
1975, writing about Mother Teresa and her work, McNamara stated:

> More important than the organisational structure of her work
> is the message it conveys that genuine peace is not the mere
> absence of hostilities, but rather that tranquility that arises out
> of a social order in which individuals treat one another with
> justice and compassion. The long history of human conflict
> suggests that without greater recognition of that fact—a fact
> which Mother Teresa's concern for the absolute poor strikingly
> so illustrates—the prospects for world peace will remain per-
> ilously fragile.[3]

Then, on October 16, 1979, came the announcement that many had
waited for: the Nobel committee awarded the 1979 Nobel Peace Prize to
Mother Teresa. In the wake of the pronouncement, some nagging questions remained. Why, for instance, did the committee choose Mother
Teresa this time and not others? Who had, in fact, nominated her? But because the committee's meetings are kept secret, no one will ever know
what took place during the deliberations for the award.

Meanwhile, in Calcutta, Mother Teresa was mobbed when the news
was announced. Journalists and photographers jostled one another as they
tried to talk to Mother Teresa to get her reaction to the good news. Standing in front of the Motherhouse, she spoke to the gathering media about
the news, stating "I am unworthy. I accept the prize in the name of the
poor. The prize is the recognition of the poor world. . . . By serving the poor
I am serving him." A reception was held in her honor in which one official proclaimed, "You have been the mother of Bengal and now you are
the mother of the world."[4] That same day, a small abandoned baby girl was
brought into the Shishu Bhavan in Calcutta. She was named Shanti,
which means "Peace" in Hindi, in honor of Mother Teresa's award.

The celebrations had just begun. Over the next few days, Mother
Teresa received more than 500 telegrams from heads of state all over the

world. Letters of praise and congratulations also poured in. Many people stopped by Motherhouse to offer their congratulations and best wishes. Many in India rejoiced that the prize had once again come to their country; six decades earlier, the Nobel committee had awarded the same prize to Mahatma Gandhi. The government also issued a commemorative postage stamp in Mother Teresa's honor. Many people rejoiced around the world, that, for once, the Nobel committee had put politics to the side and picked a true humanitarian, one who easily matched the stature of previous winners such as Albert Schweitzer, Gandhi, and Martin Luther King, Jr. Other people believed that by winning the Nobel Peace Prize, Mother Teresa had enhanced the prestige of the award.

Still, there were detractors. Some of the most vocal dissent came from an extremist anti-Gandhian group that published an article "Nothing Noble about the Nobel":

> For when all is said and done, she is a missionary. In serving the poor and the sick, her sole objective is to influence people in favour of Christianity and, if possible to convert them. Missionaries are instruments of Western imperialist countries— and not innocent voices of God.[5]

Another critic wrote to *The New York Times* stating that his understanding of the Nobel Peace Prize was that it was to be given to an individual who made important contributions to world peace, not to someone who merely helped individuals in distress. Another article, in the *National Catholic Reporter*, suggested that Mother Teresa and her Missionaries of Charity merely covered the wounds left by capitalism and that they did little in the way of actually helping to change the conditions that make people poor. In general, the hubbub over Mother Teresa's winning of the prize overshadowed the winners of the other Nobel prizes that year.

## ON TO OSLO

In December 1979, Mother Teresa, accompanied by four other nuns, traveled to Oslo to receive the Nobel Prize medal and a check for £90,000 (appx. $161,000). In addition, there was another check of £36,000 (appx. $64,000) awaiting her, which was a donation raised by the young people of Norway. Another £3,000 (appx. $5,300) was later presented to her after she requested that the monies spent on the customary banquet given in honor of the recipient instead be given to those who needed a meal more.

It was a bitterly cold day and many people in the audience were bundled up in fur coats and hats in the Aula Magna of Oslo University where Mother Teresa was slated to give her remarks and receive her prize. In the crowd were the king and crown princess of Norway, along with many other world dignitaries. The stage was banked with lush floral arrangements; nearby, a symphony orchestra played selections from Edvard Grieg, the great Norwegian composer. Wearing only a gray cardigan sweater and black coat over her thin cotton sari, Mother Teresa made her way to the podium. After asking her audience to join her in prayer, she then began her speech. According to the reporter for the magazine *National Review,* Mother Teresa's speech was not only on the poor, but on abortion, stating that nations who allowed legalized abortions are really the poorest of all. She further argued that the most horrendous crime of all existed "against the innocent unborn child."[6]

Another journalist wrote that Mother Teresa went on to state:

> I feel that the greatest destroyer of peace today is abortion. Because it is a direct war, a direct killing—direct murder by the mother herself.... Because if a mother can kill her own child—what is left but for me to kill you and you to kill me—there is nothing in between.[7]

Mother Teresa also spoke of the great spiritual poverty of the West:

> Around the world, not only in the poor countries, I found the poverty of the West so much more difficult to remove.... a person that has been thrown out from society—that poverty is so hurtful and so much, that I find it very difficult. Our Sisters are working amongst that kind of people in the West.[8]

Even though the Norwegian paper *Aftenposten* commented how the press was spellbound by the tiny nun who won the award, there were numerous others who were critical of her remarks. In the aftermath of her speech, one thing was clear: Mother Teresa had not only stated her view of abortion, but also made it clear she would not change her views. And when given the opportunity, she would speak out on the subject to any who would listen.

As if the abortion issue were not controversial enough, Mother Teresa disappointed many Albanians with her comments on the religious persecution in Albania. When asked by a reporter for her thoughts on the subject, Mother Teresa demurred, stating that she could not say much because she did not know what was going on. But, as more than one critic has pointed out, the fact that she was in contact with her mother and sister until they died, along with her repeated attempts to get them out of the country, or at least to gain permission to visit, demonstrate that Mother Teresa, in fact, knew well the conditions present in the country. In addition, earlier that year, Mother Teresa had met with the widow of the Albanian king, Queen Geraldine, when the country's predicament surely would have been discussed.

In the wake of the Nobel Prize ceremonies, many of Mother Teresa's supporters stated that she did not comment on the Albanian question because she refused to become involved in any controversial political stances, as that was incompatible with her primary mission: helping the poor. But her detractors point out that, by making her comments on abortion, Mother Teresa was in fact involving herself in what was clearly one of the most heated political arguments of the day.

## DAPHNE RAE AND *LOVE UNTIL IT HURTS*

Following Mother Teresa's winning of the Nobel Prize, activity at the Motherhouse at 54A Lower Circular Road picked up considerably. Offers and donations poured in from all over the world, as many companies and individuals offered to help the Missionaries of Charity. From Bata Shoe Company came leather for leprosy patients to make shoes. Help the Aged, a nonprofit organization based in England, donated money for meals. An international organization, the Rotary Club, also pledged money and help for Mother Teresa. Also aiding Mother Teresa in her work were many wealthy individuals who gave both time and money for the poor.

One of these volunteers was Daphne Rae, who came to Calcutta to work in the slums. Rae was the wife of the headmaster of Westminster, one of the best schools in England. Rae, originally from Sri Lanka, converted to Catholicism in 1977 and came to Calcutta in 1979, leaving her husband and six children to work with Mother Teresa. Altogether, she traveled to the city three times in order to work with the Missionaries of Charity. She brought with her large donations of medical supplies and medicines and spent much of her time at Nirmal Hriday and the children's home. But, suddenly, Rae stopped working with Mother Teresa, and instead devoted her energy to working with lesser-known organizations also dedicated to helping India's poor.

Although she never publicly stated why she no longer worked with the Missionaries of Charity, Rae's 1981 book, *Love until It Hurts: Mother*

*Teresa and Her Missionaries of Charity,* offers some clues about her change of heart. Rae, who had previously worked with the terminally ill and dying, was no stranger to places such as Nirmal Hriday. However, she was distressed that while helping Mother Teresa, she saw disposable hypodermic needles used over and over again; in some cases as many as 40 or 50 times.

Rae, who was also a passionate opponent of abortion, was bothered by the approach the nuns took toward single, pregnant mothers at the Shishu Bhavan. For a young, unmarried Hindu girl to become pregnant was a scandal, and for many, abortion was often seen as the only solution. For those unwilling to terminate their pregnancy, there was the possibility of sanctuary at the Shishu Bhavan. Often these girls were taken in by the nuns with the understanding that they would receive a place to sleep, medical care, and help in placing the infant up for adoption in return for helping with domestic chores. According to Rae, these arrangements in fact often resulted in the girls being treated as the lowliest form of servant with only the barest of necessities provided for them. She also found a kind of moral superiority on the part of the nuns, certainly not in keeping with the charitable expressions toward unmarried women espoused in public by the order.

## A WOMAN IN DEMAND

Beginning in the 1980s, Mother Teresa stepped up her visits, traveling all over the world to meet with world leaders or to open another foundation somewhere for the Missionaries of Charity. Her travels kept her away from Motherhouse even more; it was usual for her to be gone for 10 months out of every year. At the behest of Pope John Paul II, with whom she developed a very close relationship, Mother Teresa used her travels and the media attention to air her views, giving her a platform second to none among religious leaders.

The new decade opened with Mother Teresa traveling again to her hometown of Skopje as a guest of the city. Months earlier, she also had the opportunity to open a house for the elderly in Zagreb, Croatia, marking the first time the Missionaries of Charity had opened one of their homes in a communist country. She attended a conference on family life in Guatemala; then went to visit the desperately poor island of Haiti, where she met the then-president Jean-Claude "Baby Doc" Duvalier and his wife. From Haiti, she traveled to Egypt where, much to the Egyptian government's dismay, she urged Egyptian housewives to have many children. The government, which had just finished producing a series of short films that urged families to limit the number of children, could do nothing.

In addition to Mother Teresa's traveling, the Missionaries of Charity opened a number of new facilities throughout the world. In 1980, 14 new homes were opened; in 1981, 18. Twelve Missionaries of Charity foundations opened in 1982; in 1983, the number rose to 14. At the beginning of the decade, the Missionaries of Charity established 140 slum schools, a daily meal program that fed nearly 50,000 persons at 304 centers. There were 70 Shishu Bhavans, which took care of approximately 4,000 children, out of which 1,000 adoptions were arranged. There were 81 homes for the dying and 670 mobile clinics that had treated some 6 million patients. Although the Missionaries of Charity were going global with their work, the bulk of their endeavors were still based in India.

Mother Teresa also continued to show little regard for her own personal safety as she ventured into many of the world's hotspots. In 1982, she went to West Beirut where the area's hospitals had been shelled by Israeli artillery. While there, she took 37 children who had been stranded in a mental hospital on a Red Cross convoy into East Beirut and safety. In 1984, she traveled to Bhopal, India, where a poisonous gas leak at a Union Carbide plant killed thousands of people and left many others in terrible health.

During this period, Mother Teresa also plunged into the growing AIDS crisis. She opened a hospice in Greenwich Village in New York City to care for patients who were suffering from what she termed as the new leprosy of the West. Among her first patients were three convicts suffering from the disease in the notorious Sing-Sing Prison near New York City. But despite her willingness to tackle the deadly disease and provide hospice care, Mother Teresa was criticized for her handling of AIDs patients. According to one account, a doctor who was also working at the hospice was appalled by how little the nuns knew about the disease. The doctor told Mother Teresa that simply wearing a crucifix around her neck offered her no protection from the disease. To this, Mother Teresa replied that God would take care of her. But for critics this argument was flawed at best, and dangerous at worst, as the account illustrates: "God never provides knowledge or skill. God in fact is never enough.... [T]he teresan community sees it [AIDS] as a sickness that can be assuaged with loving words and a little hot soup."[9]

## THE SAINT AND THE SINNER

In 1985 came one of the oddest pairings the world had seen: that of a young, anti-Catholic Irish rock musician and the tiny nun who worked with the world's poor. On the face of it, the idea of rock star Bob Geldof, lead singer of the Boomtown Rats, meeting with Mother Teresa not only seemed odd; it was completely incongruous. But the two actually had something in common: working to help the poor.

Geldof, an Irish Catholic who had little use for the Church of his youth, had come to the forefront during 1984 for his concert Band Aid to raise money for the poor in Africa. In 1985, he was traveling to Ethiopia to help distribute the funds raised. He met Mother Teresa at the Addis Ababa airport in January 1985. Geldof remembered, upon greeting her, how tiny she was. He towered more than two feet above her. He described her as a battered, wizened woman whose most striking characteristic was her feet. Mother Teresa's sandals were beaten up pieces of leather; her feet were gnarled and misshapen. When Geldof tried to kiss her, Mother Teresa bowed her head quickly so that he could only kiss the top of her wimple. This bothered Geldof a great deal. He later found out that she only let lepers kiss her.

As photographers snapped their picture, Mother Teresa and Geldof began talking, she about the Missionaries of Charity, he about his band, the Boomtown Rats. He even offered to arrange a benefit concert for her work. But she gently refused him, stating that God would provide for her. As Geldof later recounted, he had an opportunity to see Providence in action. Upon arriving in the city, Mother Teresa had seen some vacant buildings and asked if she could have the buildings to use as orphanages. Flummoxed government officials, not wanting to turn her down, clearly did not know what to do. But it was clear that Mother Teresa knew about the buildings beforehand. When the official told her he would find her a building for her orphanages, she reminded him that she needed two buildings for two orphanages, not one.

When asked later for his impression of Mother Teresa, Geldof replied that she was the embodiment of moral good, but also added that there was nothing otherworldly about her. She showed herself fully capable of handling the media and could manipulate them easily. He also found her devoid of any false modesty or pretense; she was totally selfless in her work and seemed genuinely to care about the people she was helping.

In 1986, Mother Teresa made further headlines when she traveled to the Soviet Union to meet with government officials. Two years later, she returned with four nuns to begin working in a Moscow hospital helping victims of an earthquake. Her visit was unprecedented and marked the first time that a religious mission was allowed to open a house since the Russian Revolution in 1917.

## AN UNHAPPY VISIT

In 1988, Mother Teresa traveled to London to visit with Prime Minister Margaret Thatcher. She also visited Cardboard City, the site of the city's homeless. She asked Thatcher for help in setting up a hostel for them, but Thatcher pointed out that there were voluntary organizations in the city that specifically worked with the homeless, and there was no need for Mother Teresa's help.

There were other problems as well. Mother Teresa's trip coincided with a hearing in Parliament for a bill that would reduce the time limit for allowing abortions from the current 28 weeks to 18 weeks. Mother Teresa again went to Thatcher asking her to support the bill. Again she was refused. At a conference in Oxford, Mother Teresa told the audience that couples who used contraception other than the rhythm method, as allowed by the Catholic Church, would not be accepted as potential adoptive parents for any children coming from the Missionaries of Charity homes.

Shortly afterward, Mother Teresa met with Robert Maxwell, the Australian owner of the London newspaper the *Daily Mirror*. Maxwell, already known for his dubious business dealings, offered to help raise money for a new Missionaries of Charity home in London. Maxwell loved the publicity, and Mother Teresa, either in the dark about Maxwell's personal business dealings or refusing to acknowledge them, accepted his offer. It also allowed her a chance to do something without going through government channels. In all, £169,000 (appx. $302,000) was raised and deposited in an account held by Maxwell and the paper. In addition, another £90,000 (appx. $160,000) was raised by the readers of a Scottish paper to be used for Mother Teresa's efforts. With the funds, she hoped to set up two facilities for the homeless in London.

But Mother Teresa never saw the money. Some speculated that Maxwell had appropriated the funds. A spokesman for the *Daily Mirror* later charged that Mother Teresa never seemed to find an appropriate home or piece of land to suit her purposes. He further denied that any of the money was missing. There was also the stigma attached of having accepted the money in the first place from a man who was a known swindler and unsavory businessman. If Mother Teresa had any regrets about any of her actions, her association with Maxwell was one. Finally, though, in 1993, a 35-room hostel was opened in London for the Missionaries of Charity. Mother Teresa came for the opening ceremony and once again thanked readers of the *Daily Mirror* for their generosity. Mother Teresa complained, though, that officials of the British government did little to ease the suffering of homeless in their country, despite her offers of help.

Although the last 20 years had brought great recognition for Mother Teresa and her organization, it was also a period of loss, regret, and controversy. With a new decade looming before her, Mother Teresa, at the age of 80, showed no signs of slowing down. However, the coming years would be less than kind to her, both personally and professionally, as she strove to continue her work with the poor.

## NOTES

1. Kathryn Spink, *Mother Teresa* (San Francisco: Harper & Row, 1997), p. 102.

2. Germaine Greer, "Heroes and Villains," *Independent*, September 22, 1990.

3. Raghu Rai and Navin Chawla, *Mother Teresa: Faith and Compassion* (Rockport, Mass.: Element, 1992), p. 184; Anne Sebba, *Mother Teresa: Beyond the Image* (New York: Doubleday, 1997), p. 100.

4. Eileen Egan, *Such a Vision of the Street: Mother Teresa—The Spirit and the Work* (Garden City, N.Y.: Image Books, 1986), p. 396.

5. Egan, *Vision*, p. 398.

6. "The Week," *National Review*, January 4, 1980, p. 12.

7. Nobel Foundation, "Mother Teresa Nobel Lecture," http://www.nobel.se/peace/laureates/1979/teresa-lecture.html (accessed November 19, 2003).

8. Nobel Foundation, "Mother Teresa Nobel Lecture," http://www.nobel.se/peace/laureates/1979/teresa-lecture.html (accessed November 19, 2003).

9. Anthony Burgess, "Mother Teresa," *Evening Standard*, January 3, 1992.

# Chapter 10

# "THE MOST OBEDIENT WOMAN IN THE CHURCH"

Even though Mother Teresa kept up her busy schedule, it was clear by the early 1990s that traveling from place to place, visiting many of the world's most troubled spots, could not last forever. Beginning in 1989, her health began deteriorating. In September of that year, she suffered a near-fatal heart attack and underwent major surgery. The heart trouble was not new; she had first been diagnosed with it almost 15 years earlier. Still, she continued her frenetic pace.

After being fitted with a pacemaker in December 1989, Mother Teresa traveled to establish new homes for the Missionaries of Charity. But in 1991, she was hospitalized again, this time at the Scripps Clinic and Research Foundation in La Jolla, California, where she was treated for heart disease and bacterial pneumonia. Later, she took ill while visiting in Tijuana, Mexico, and doctors were forced to perform surgery to open a blood vessel.

Although increasingly frail, Mother Teresa did not slow down. Then, in 1993, while in Rome, she fell and broke her ribs. That July, she was hospitalized for two days in Bombay for exhaustion; not more than a month later, she was back in the hospital in New Delhi, this time for a malarial infection, which was further complicated by heart and lung problems. She was transferred to the All India Institute of Medical Sciences, where she recuperated in the intensive-care coronary unit. She was home in Calcutta for less than a month, when she was treated by doctors yet again, this time for a blocked heart vessel. Clearly, age and the years of deprivation, travel, and work were taking their toll on Mother Teresa's health.

## UNWILLING TO LET GO

By 1990, given her ill health, Mother Teresa began giving serious thought to stepping down as head of the Missionaries of Charity. She even went as far as to inform Pope John Paul II of her intentions. Yet, she did nothing. Some people believed that Mother Teresa did not wish to relinquish control of the order she had founded. Others thought that she feared a sudden drop in donations if she stepped down. Therefore, it was crucial to the survival of the order and their mission that she remain at the helm.

Even among her supporters, Mother Teresa's refusal to appoint a successor was troubling. For many, building up what had become a major institution with a tremendous amount of goodwill and money, but not looking ahead to the future seemed short-sighted and egocentric. Church leaders were also concerned; clearly, it was time for a younger, more vigorous leader to take over the order. Mother Teresa's supporters also feared that the great goodwill she had built up would somehow be negated by her ill health. One supporter, working in the Vatican, also believed that, even if she stepped down, Mother Teresa would still stay involved in the order. She could concentrate on things such as the daily administration and education, which did not require the exhaustive traveling that she did. For the time being, Mother Teresa would not consider even a partial retirement.

Thus, despite her ill health, Mother Teresa continued to respond to new crises around the world. She also continued to receive large financial donations from world leaders. For instance, Yassir Arafat, head of the Palestinian Liberation Organization, presented her personally with a $50,000 check in Calcutta, though he never commented on why he made such a generous donation to the Missionaries of Charity.

The last three decades had for the most part been very kind to Mother Teresa. She enjoyed public acclaim and was handled gently by the media. But the attitudes changed in the 1990s. Signaling the perceptible shift was the publication of Germaine Greer's article about Mother Teresa's efforts in Bangladesh almost 20 years earlier. There was also trouble when it was announced that a movie of Mother Teresa's life was being planned. Slated to play her was British actress Glenda Jackson and the script was being written by Dominique LaPierre, who had written the best-selling book *City of Joy*, which described working with Missionaries of Charity. The proposed film even had the Vatican's support; yet Mother Teresa declined to cooperate with the film project and never explained her decision. Newspaper and magazine profiles of her were now often less flattering, portraying her as demanding and egotistical. This was only portent of what lay ahead.

## HELL'S ANGEL

On November 8, 1994, the switchboard operator at the British television station Channel Four was bombarded by over 200 calls. Many of the callers were irate viewers who had just finished watching a half-hour film called *Hell's Angel*, produced by Pakistani-born Tariq Ali, a noted and controversial author and broadcaster. The angel was Mother Teresa, and the tempest surrounding the film, already generating controversy in previews, showed no sign of cooling down soon.

The film, which featured journalist Christopher Hitchens, made some accusations, many of which had been noted earlier by the British-born Hitchens in his writings for such well-known publications as *Vanity Fair* and the ultraliberal news magazine *Nation*. Among the many inflammatory statements Hitchens made was that "Mother Teresa has an easy way with thrones, dominions and powers," and operated "as the roving ambassador of [the] highly politicized papacy"[1] of Pope John Paul II. In addition, Hitchens charged that Mother Teresa

> lends spiritual solace to dictators and to wealthy exploiters, which is scarcely the essence of simplicity, and she preaches surrender and prostration to the poor, which a truly humble person would barely have the nerve to do.... In a godless and cynical age it may be inevitable that people will seek to praise the self-effacing, the altruistic and the pure in heart. But only a complete collapse of our critical faculties can explain the illusion that such a person is manifested in the shape of a demagogue, an obscurantist and a servant of earthly powers.[2]

The source of the film was actually Dr. Aroup Chatterjee, a Bengali physician living in London. Dr. Chatterjee, who was born and raised in Calcutta, was dismayed at the discrepancy between Mother Teresa's work and the growing cult-like adulation of her in the West. In a letter written to the production company Bandung, Dr. Chatterjee also stated that Mother Teresa's assets totaled more than those of many Third-World governments; and that in Calcutta, unlike the West, she was regarded as something of a nonentity. Chatterjee's greatest objection, though, was in how closely intertwined Mother Teresa's work and identity were with Calcutta, another misconception on the part of the West. Chatterjee pointed out that there were a number of other individuals and groups doing far more for the city's poor than the Missionaries of Charity, and these groups were completely overlooked.

The production company was more than willing to listen to Chatterjee's proposal. The company had already, in its short existence, voiced some of the very same grievances that Chatterjee had described. Calcuttans were annoyed that Western journalists and filmmakers portrayed their city as a place that cared little for the poor, the sick, and the dying. In the 1991 film *City of Joy,* for example, Calcutta was depicted as little more than a dark pit of misery and despair.

The decision to interview Hitchens might at first have seemed odd. But, in fact, he was already quite familiar with Mother Teresa, having first met her in 1980. In a 1992 article called the "Ghoul of Calcutta," Hitchens described his first encounter with Mother Teresa, whom he described as the "leathery old saint." He had stopped at the Missionaries of Charity facility on Bose Road and was immediately put off by the home's motto "He That Loveth Correction Loveth Knowledge." Despite his reaction, Hitchens agreed to go along on a walk with Mother Teresa. Initially, he was favorably impressed:

> I was about to mutter some words of praise for the nurses and was even fumbling in my pocket when Mother Teresa announced: "You see, this is how we fight abortion and contraception in Calcutta." Mother Teresa's avowed motive somewhat cheapened the ostensible work of the charity and made it appear rather more like what it actually is: an exercise in propaganda.[3]

As harsh as that initial assessment was, Hitchens had an opportunity in the film to voice even more accusations. Against footage of Mother Teresa that showed her bent and looking down, Hitchens described her connection with the deposed Haitian dictator Jean-Claude "Baby Doc" Duvalier, from whom she accepted large financial donations. Footage was also shown of her laying a wreath at the grave of Enver Hoxha, the ruthless communist dictator of Albania, and meeting with notorious figures in the business world. According to Hitchens, Mother Teresa's Missionaries of Charity grossed an annual income in the neighborhood of tens of millions of dollars.

Hitchens also suggested, as had some of Mother Teresa's other critics, that if the monies accumulated by the order were kept in Calcutta, chances are the order would certainly make much more of a difference in working with the poor. Instead, Mother Teresa spread her nuns and their money very thinly trying to open homes throughout the world. Further, Hitchens argued, Mother Teresa chose her convent and the church's teachings over the work of her clinics.

According to the BBC, the Channel Four program did spectacularly: approximately 1.6 million viewers tuned in to watch. In the aftermath of the documentary's airing, callers phoning the station called the program insulting, hurtful, offensive, obscene, untrue, obnoxious, shocking, and satanic. One viewer even went so far as to accuse the head of the station, Michael Grade, a Jew, of anti-Catholic bias, while both Hitchens and Tariq Ali were branded as Bolsheviks and Marxist revolutionaries. Other viewers believe the film was nothing less than the work of a Judeo-Muslim conspiracy.

The Roman Catholic Church understandably rallied to Mother Teresa's defense, denouncing the program as a grotesque caricature of the woman and her work. Noted Catholic writer and historian Paul Johnson called the documentary a diabolical and malicious attack by left-wing pro-pagandists. Another 130 viewers went so far as to lodge a complaint with the Independent Television Commission, which, after considering the matter, refused to sanction the station for broadcasting the film.

In Calcutta, several of Mother Teresa's supporters rallied to her cause, calling the film biased. As of 2004, the film has yet to be shown in India, due in part to how expensive the film is to sell, though copies are available privately. Mother Teresa was undeterred by the controversy surrounding her. When asked about the film in an interview, she simply stated, "No matter who says what, you should accept it with a smile and do your own work."[4] However, the day after the program was shown, she did cancel a scheduled visit to Taiwan, but did not explain her reasons for doing so to anyone.

Despite the backlash against the film and Hitchens, there were those who applauded what the film tried to do. One reviewer writing for the *Guardian* stated that Hitchens was completely right in questioning what he called the "cult of Teresa." Another supporter of the program was the Reverend Andrew de Berry, who had met Mother Teresa many years earlier when he was a chaplain-in-training. He recalled her telling an audience that she advised the women of Calcutta to have as many children as they wanted. De Berry then wrote that the experience stayed with him always; and undoubtedly many who died on the streets of Calcutta were the children of mothers who took Mother Teresa's counsel.

## THE MISSIONARY POSITION

After *Hell's Angel* Hitchens published a small book that picked up where the film left off. In *The Missionary Position: Mother Teresa in Theory and Practice*, Hitchens hoped to elaborate on Mother Teresa and her work, by "judging Mother Teresa's reputation by her actions and words rather than the actions and words by her reputation."[5] According to Hitchens, Mother Teresa's shining reputation was put upon her by the millions of people who needed to feel that someone, somewhere, is doing the things that they are not to help the poor. Further, Hitchens charged, Mother Teresa fed on this adoration, and, contrary to what she says, has not only come to accept it, but expects and even demands it.

Hitchens's book posed some troubling questions. Among other things, Hitchens questioned how Mother Teresa spent the money she had raised. Hitchens could find no satisfactory answer, and Mother Teresa consistently refused to discuss her financial affairs. As Hitchens stated, "The decision not to [fund a proper hospital], and to run instead a haphazard and cranky institution which would expose itself to litigation and protest were it run by any branch of the medical profession, is a deliberate one. The point is not the honest relief of suffering but the promulgation of a cult based on death and suffering and subjection."[6]

Mother Teresa's apologists have often portrayed her as an innocent who professes to know little of business and politics, and who is concerned only with God and God's will. In reality, as Hitchens points out, Mother Teresa kept some questionable company over the years. She has received hospitality, awards, publicity, and money from numerous persons with overt political motives or dubious business histories such as Robert Maxwell; the Duvaliers; President Ronald Reagan; Prime Minister Margaret Thatcher; President Bill Clinton and his wife Hillary Clinton; and Charles Keating, one of the key figures in the savings and loan scandal of the 1990s. The relationship with Keating was particularly galling. Keating made a generous donation to Mother Teresa as well as making his private jet available for her use. When Keating was imprisoned for fraud and embezzlement, Mother Teresa petitioned the trial judge to look kindly on him. When she received a reply from one of the prosecutors, explaining that the $10,000 she had received from Keating was stolen from innocent and not especially wealthy investors, Mother Teresa never answered the letter.

Hitchens maintained that such blatant and deliberate disregard for the truth on Mother Teresa's part was not a sign of naiveté or even stupidity, but rather arrogance. Claiming to be above politics, Mother Teresa also had the benefit of an almost unprecedented public forum. But while speaking out against abortion in Great Britain, Ireland, and the United States, she remained noticeably silent on the topics of unlawful deaths, murders, and oppression in such political hotspots as Ethiopia, Haiti, and Albania, where she kissed the hands of ruling dictators and willingly took their money and their awards.

Her refusal to acknowledge the deep problems of poverty emerged in Hitchens's description of a 1981 visit that Mother Teresa made to Anacostia, an African American ghetto in Washington, D.C. At that time, the Missionaries of Charity intended to establish some sort of operation there, though many of the area's residents did not want to give the impression that their neighborhood was helpless and poor like many of the Third World areas in which Mother Teresa worked. Just before a press conference, a group of African American men visited Mother Teresa:

> They were very upset.... They told Mother that Anacostia needed decent jobs, housing and services—not charity. Mother didn't argue with them; she just listened. Finally one of them asked her what she was going to do here. Mother said: "First we must learn to love one another." They didn't know what to say to that.[7]

Hitchens's book, like the film, had its detractors and admirers. George Sim Johnston, writing for the American conservative publication *The National Review*, called Hitchens's work "unresisting imbecility," and added that "the only good that will come from this book is the prayers the nuns of Mother Teresa's order are no doubt saying for its author."[8] *The New York Times Book Review* found that Hitchens's book is, "zealously overwritten, and rails wildly in defense of an almost nonsensical proposition: that Mother Teresa of Calcutta is actually not a saint but an evil and selfish old woman." Yet the reviewer concluded that Hitchens had a point: "Ultimately, he argues, Mother Teresa is less interested in helping the poor than in using them as an indefatigable source of wretchedness on which to fuel the expansion of her fundamentalist Roman Catholic beliefs."[9] The *Sunday Times* was even more succinct: "Veteran lefty kicks old nun; old nun forgives; lefty doesn't want to be forgiven."[10]

Mary Poplin, a journalist writing for *Commonweal* magazine, visited Calcutta in 1996. She was there to write about Mother Teresa and her work; she also took the opportunity to ask Mother Teresa about the Hitchens's book. According to Poplin's account, when questioned about the charge that Mother Teresa was one of the wealthiest women in the world, and that she certainly did not need any more money, Mother Teresa, after a puzzled look, replied, "Oh yes, the book. I haven't read it but some of the sisters have. It matters not, he [Hitchens] is forgiven." Poplin laughed and then said, "Yes, Mother, in the end of the book, he says he knew you said you forgave him and he's irate because he says he didn't ask you to forgive him and he didn't need it." She looked at me as though I hadn't understood, then gently and confidently instructed me, "Oh, it is not I who forgives, it is God, it is God. God forgives."[11]

## A GROWING MINORITY

The bitter arguments over Hitchens's charges in both *Hell's Angel* and *The Missionary Position* might have ended there, if it had not been for other, more moderate voices also coming forward with their criticisms of Mother Teresa. Dr. Robin Fox, a thoracic specialist and editor of the highly respected medical journal, the *Lancet*, wrote in 1994 of the poor medical facilities found at Nirmal Hriday in Calcutta. According to Fox, he was astonished to find that there were no simple testing procedures implemented to distinguish an incurable from a curable disease: "Such systematic approaches are alien to the ethos of the home.... Along with the neglect of diagnosis, the lack of good analgesia marks Mother Teresa's approach as clearly separate from the hospice movement. I know which I prefer."[12] Further, although it appeared that the poor in the facilities that the Missionaries of Charity operated could not receive even basic treatment, Mother Teresa herself had access to the most modern medical treatment in the world, especially when her heart problems came to light.

Not long after Dr. Fox's criticism appeared, a thoughtful piece by Clifford Longley, a writer and former religious affairs correspondent for the London *Times,* warned of Mother Teresa's reverence for death. Such an emphasis, Longley feared, threatened to turn suffering into a goal. In addition, many health workers who visited the clinics and listened to Mother Teresa's views on abortion wondered how anyone who concerned themselves with the problems of the poor could not also be concerned with the problems of fertility, overpopulation, and other questions of reproductive health. The furor over *Hell's Angel* had in fact opened up the debate over Mother Teresa's work during the last 50 years; for the first time, opposition to her seemed to be emerging and hardening. Was Mother Teresa's way of dealing with the poor outmoded as some of her critics charged, or, as some of her supporters suggested, would there always be the need for the kind of Christian charity Mother Teresa exemplified?

In her article "No Humanitarian," Mary Poplin who spent two months working as a volunteer, described the rough conditions of Mother Teresa's medical facilities:

> Like many Western visitors, I initially found the experience disorienting. Despite Mother Teresa's repeated reminders that the order's mission is religious, not social work, most Westerners who visit the homes for sick and handicapped children expect them to look like medical clinics or hospitals. They don't. Most shocking is the absence of hospital-like procedures and equipment. This can be particularly disconcerting for people who have worked in hospital settings in America and Europe.... Surely, given Mother Teresa's fame, such equipment was available?.... The Missionaries of Charity, one learns, resist owning anything, even medical equipment that is not widely available to the poor.[13]

## PUTTING HER HOUSE IN ORDER

By the mid-1990s, Mother Teresa was fighting not only ill health but also the growing criticism of her mission. Any ideas she may have had about retiring were now out of the question. Her seemingly contradictory actions and world fame had put her in an uncomfortable position. Yet, she also relied more fully on the advice and support of the other sisters, some of whom believed that Mother Teresa was trying to get her affairs in order.

In May 1993, Mother Teresa traveled to Belgium where she was to help celebrate a gathering of Co-Workers. Because so many volunteers were going to attend the meeting in Antwerp, they decided to hold a meeting of the governing body to discuss a Co-Worker chapter that had been planned for San Diego the following year. Many believed the gathering in Antwerp would be a good opportunity to address the organization about some of her concerns.

Mother Teresa was scheduled to speak on May 8; however, the evening before, Brother Geoff, General Servant of the Missionary Brothers, announced to the assembly that allegations had been made against the Co-Workers for misuse of funds; monies that should have gone to the poor were thought instead to have been spent on Co-Workers' travel expenses, newsletters, and postage. He then informed the stunned audience that Mother Teresa was going to dissolve the Co-Workers organization the next day and cancel the San Diego chapter.

The announcement came as a terrible shock to the group. But for those who had been with Mother Teresa almost from the beginning, her actions were in character. For those volunteers, working with Mother Teresa had always been a bit of a balancing act: on one hand, she could raise enormous amounts of money for the poor; on the other, she had no problem telling the Co-Workers that they could not make Christmas cards in order to raise money. This attitude formed the crux of Mother Teresa's own concern over money; namely that it would become too central a preoccupation for the organization and its volunteers. First and foremost, the work was always to be about the poor. In the end, with the help of Brother Geoff, the Co-Workers convinced Mother Teresa not to disband the group.

Plagued by her physical ailments, Mother Teresa battled memory lapses, confusion, and a growing dependency on others. She no longer was as accessible as she had been in years past. For many volunteers, there was the question of whether these changes were hampering her judgment and influencing what they perceived as erratic behavior and inconsistent decisions. Her supporters, however, maintained that Mother Teresa was simply reminding her volunteers not to lose track of their priorities: to live a simple life and maintain a deep spirituality and faith in God.

In September 1993, Mother Teresa received sad news; Father Van Exem, the priest who had reluctantly agreed to serve as her spiritual advisor over 50 years ago, had died. His death was a terrible blow to Mother Teresa for the two had become close friends. Because she was still recovering from her own illness, she could not attend his funeral, but watched sadly from her bedroom window as the funeral procession made its way to St. John's Cemetery for burial.

Shortly before his death, Father Van Exem wrote to Mother Teresa, telling her that he would be offering his prayers for the following intercessions: that she would recover from her latest illness of a blocked heart vessel without surgery; that she would travel to China by October of that year; and that God would take him, instead of her. And so it was at the end of October that Mother Teresa arrived in China to arrange for the opening of a home for children. Her visit was a quick one; she stopped in Shanghai and Beijing before going to Rome and then to Poland. She returned to China once more in March 1994 with the hope of opening a house for handicapped children. Her wish to establish the Missionaries of Charity failed; China, by 1994, was becoming less open and Mother Teresa turned her energies elsewhere.

## MORE CONTROVERSY

Mother Teresa's final years were touched by controversy. In February 1994, she attended a National Prayer Breakfast in Washington, D.C. She did so reluctantly, having been invited by then-President Bill Clinton. She had been asked to speak and did so with much of her speech focusing on the topic of abortion. However, when she was finished, no one at the top table where the president was sitting applauded, though President Clinton later apologized. Mother Teresa did meet Hillary Clinton, who traveled with her daughter, Chelsea, to Calcutta the following year to visit one of the Missionary of Charity homes. With Mrs. Clinton's help, a children's shelter operated by the order opened in Washington in June 1995.

Two other unhappy events in Calcutta ensnared Mother Teresa. In September 1995, a 15-year-old girl who lived on the city streets was cooking a meal. She overturned the fire and was badly burned. A local doctor found her some days later lying outside with third-degree burns and severe damage to one arm. He managed to get the young woman into a state hospital, but it became difficult to obtain the right medications for her. Her relatives removed her and she went back to living on the street. After a month, her wounds became severely infected and so her relatives searched for another facility.

By this time, the local press had gotten wind of the story. The Missionaries of Charity were contacted and they agreed to send an ambulance for the girl. She was first taken to Nirmal Hriday, but was turned away because she was not dying. The next stop was to Shishu Bhavan, where she was turned away again, having been told that she was not an orphan and moreover was married with a child. Her next destination was Prem Dan, but again she was refused admission because she was not suffering from tuberculosis nor was she insane. In the end, the burn victim was deposited back on the street.

The story was a sensation and marked the first time any reporting carried a strong bias against Mother Teresa. One reporter asked Mother Teresa about the young woman's predicament. To his astonishment, Mother Teresa said that she would not discuss the issue. Some told the reporter that the girl should have been in a hospital, not in one of Mother Teresa's homes. But, as the reporter later stated, his intent was never to ask Mother Teresa to take the girl, but to ask her why—when she had purportedly never refused anyone care or help—she would not admit the girl to one of her facilities. The young girl was eventually taken to another state hospital, but the story had done damage and for many caused considerable disillusionment with both Mother Teresa and the Missionaries of Charity.

Not more than two months later, Mother Teresa again became embroiled in controversy, this time of a political nature. This incident also was the first time Church officials in India publicly criticized her, and where she faced the most sustained opposition to her work and philosophy. The situation was one of the few times in which Mother Teresa became involved in a contentious row that had severe international repercussions.

## MOTHER TERESA AND THE DALITS

On November 18, 1995, Mother Teresa held special prayers at the Sacred Heart Cathedral in New Delhi. The occasion was to launch a two-week fast and protest campaign demanding scheduled caste recognition for Christian Dalits. Caste is an important part of Indian society; it is not only a declaration of social status, it determines the course of a person's life. People born into the highest caste of Indian society were those with property, money, education, and opportunities. The lowest level of Indian society were the Dalits or "untouchables."

In India alone, close to 160 million so-called Dalits, or known legally as scheduled castes, were routinely discriminated against, denied access to land, forced to work in degrading conditions, and routinely abused, even killed, at the hands of the police and of higher-caste groups that enjoyed the state's protection. The discrimination against and segregation of the Dalits has been called India's "hidden apartheid," and entire villages in many Indian states remain completely segregated by caste.

Although the practice of "untouchability" was abolished under India's constitution in 1950, social discrimination against a person or group by reason of birth into a particular caste remains very much a part of rural India. Untouchables may not cross the line dividing their part of the village from that occupied by members of the higher castes. They may not use the same wells, visit the same temples, drink from the same cups in tea stalls, or lay claim to land that is legally theirs. Dalit children are frequently made to sit in the back of classrooms, and Dalit women are frequent victims of sexual abuse. Most Dalits continue to live in extreme poverty, without land or opportunities for better employment or education. With the exception of a minority who have benefited from India's policy of quotas in education and government jobs, Dalits are relegated to the most menial of tasks, as manual scavengers, removers of human waste and dead animals, leather workers, street sweepers, and cobblers. Dalit children make up the majority of those sold into bondage to pay off debts to upper-caste creditors.

It was the government provision that allowed a small number of Dalits access to government jobs that set off the firestorm. But Dalits who had converted to Christianity were denied this opportunity on the grounds that once a person converted to Christianity, the issue of caste is no longer important. It was also argued that Christian Dalits had other opportunities available such as studying in Christian schools. Christian Dalits argued that, in using these educational facilities, they were being denied the country's resources that as citizens they should have access to. But, as others argued, if Dalits are Christians, they cannot be Dalits, as Christianity does not recognize the notion of caste. If they are Dalits, then they are Hindus, and, as far as Mother Teresa was concerned, she had little to do with them.

Mother Teresa's involvement with the campaign had tremendous repercussions. Accused of trying to introduce the pattern of caste systems into Christianity at the expense of non-Christian Dalits, Mother Teresa called a press conference in which she stated that she had no idea what the prayer meeting was about. Her statements infuriated the organization sponsoring the event. The organization secretary stated that, in fact, Mother Teresa did know the purpose of the prayer meeting as it had been explained to her by the auxiliary bishop of the Delhi archdiocese.

In another time, an incident such as this would have rallied Mother Teresa's supporters. Instead, she not only antagonized non-Christians, but Christians as well. One church official went so far as to say that Mother Teresa, with her antiquated views on abortion and family planning, had become obsolete. She had, in fact, helped create a greater schism in a country already plagued by numerous divisions.

## STEPPING ASIDE

On March 13, 1997, the Missionaries of Charity took a long-awaited step: choosing a successor to head their order. The announcement ended months of speculation not only about Mother Teresa's future, but about who would succeed her. The discussions over the new leader had been deadlocked for weeks as the order struggled to find an acceptable replacement. Eventually the members were forced to turn to Pope John Paul II who offered a compromise: Mother Teresa would stay on as spiritual and titular head of the Missionaries of Charity, while Sister Nirmala, a 63-year-old member of the order would take over the day-to-day duties of the group. It was also decided that she would hold the post for six years when the group would meet again to choose either a new head or reelect Sister Nirmala.

Despite the effort at compromise, the transition did not go smoothly. Within hours of Sister Nirmala's appointment, Mother Teresa announced plans to create a number of new homes. Sister Nirmala did not object. She was by temperament timid, and decided to maintain a low profile, even bypassing the title of "Mother" for the time being. Mother Teresa acted as if she were still in charge, while giving her blessing to her successor.

Though her health was failing, Mother Teresa continued to travel, to raise funds, and visit many of the new homes that the Missionaries of Charity established. But in March 1996, she fell out of bed and broke her collarbone. Yet, by June, she was traveling again, though she fell once more, this time severely spraining her ankle. In the meantime, her memory grew worse and lapses became more frequent.

In August 1996, Mother Teresa was once more admitted to the Woodland's Nursing Home in Calcutta. She was having trouble breathing and many believed that she was going to die. She rallied, though, and left the facility on September 6, against her doctors' wishes. She then attended special services marking the fiftieth anniversary of the founding of the Missionaries of Charity. But two weeks later, she was back in the hospital after having fallen down the stairs at the Motherhouse. More of her days were spent in bed suffering from severe back pain.

Finally, in January 1997, Mother Teresa announced her decision to resign as mother superior of the order; her health was too precarious, and even she seemed to realize that she could no longer battle her ailments as she once had. However, in May, she did travel to Rome where she met with the pope and then to the United States where she was awarded the Congressional Medal of Freedom in recognition for her work. She also made time to tour New York City's the Bronx with Princess Diana.

The untimely death of Princess Diana three months later was one more loss to bear. Mother Teresa had become good friends with the young princess, often offering her advice. The two also talked of Mother Teresa's work, and Princess Diana had made a point of visiting Nirmal Hriday when she came to India, years before. Mother Teresa's remarks on the princess' death were in fact her last public statements. On September 5, 1997, the eve of Diana's funeral, Mother Teresa's heart finally stopped. After a private service at the chapel of the Motherhouse, her body was transferred to a Missionary of Charity ambulance with the word "Mother" written across it, and taken to St. Thomas Church, which was used by the Loreto Sisters. Here, thousands of mourners crowded among the pews to pay their respects to the tiny nun. A week later, the Indian government held a state funeral for Mother Teresa. On September 13, her body was carried through the streets of Calcutta on the same gun carriage used to transport two of India's greatest leaders and heroes: Mahatma Gandhi and Jawaharlal Nehru. Thousands of mourners lined the streets as the carriage traveled to the Calcutta sports stadium where a state funeral mass was held; numerous dignitaries were in attendance to pay their respects. Afterwards, in a private ceremony, with soldiers firing their guns in a last tribute, Mother Teresa was laid to rest beneath a plain stone slab on the grounds of the Motherhouse located at A.J.C. Bose Road. Here, she is not far from the people she served and helped.

## THE MAKING OF A SAINT

Six years after her death, Mother Teresa was back in the news. In 2003, it was announced that John Paul II, to help commemorate his 25th anniversary of his election to the papacy, would beatify Mother Teresa on October 19. The event marks the final step before canonization, or official sainthood. It was a remarkable process in that no one has ever been beatified in so short a time as Mother Teresa. Yet, Vatican officials worked rigorously to treat her case as they would any other.

Even before her death, some officials in the Vatican thought she ought to be canonized without the usual investigation. Pope John Paul II even waived the usual five-year waiting period to see whether a candidate's reputation for holiness is justified. For Father Brian Kolodiejchuk, the task ahead was even more daunting; he was charged with coordinating the team that eventually put together 67 volumes arguing that Mother Teresa met all the requirements for sainthood. In addition, the church lawyers held 14 tribunals all over the world to hear testimony from people who knew Mother Teresa well. Nearly all were friendly witnesses who had to answer 263 questions that were used as evidence that Mother Teresa had manifested the virtues required of a Roman Catholic saint: faith, hope, and charity, as well as humility, prudence, justice, fortitude, and temperance to an extraordinary degree. Mother Teresa also had her critics: three non-Catholics testified against her, among them Christopher Hitchens.

In the end, Father Kolodiejchuk's team concluded that Mother Teresa's willingness to work with those who were morally and financially corrupt was in keeping with her own philosophy: using ill-gotten money to do good for the poor and also provide spiritual benefits for the donors. As to her failure to take a more aggressive stance against institutionalized injustice, the team sided with Mother Teresa. They argued that her mission was to help individuals and bear witness to the Divine presence in the world, not fight for social change.

As with all candidates for sainthood, the church required a divine sign in the form of a posthumous miracle. Many claims were submitted; the one chosen concerned a Hindu mother, Monika Besra, who came to the sisters suffering from a life-threatening stomach tumor. The sisters prayed to Mother Teresa for a cure and pressed a religious medal that she had touched to Besra's abdomen. Five hours later, the tumor had completely disappeared.

The beatification ceremonies in Rome were only the beginning of a media and merchandising frenzy surrounding Mother Teresa's eventual canonization. In Calcutta, Mother Teresa's legacy was to be honored with an international festival of films. The event was a first; no saint in the history of the Catholic Church has had an international festival of films held in their honor. Among the films scheduled to be shown were Malcolm Muggeridge's *Something Beautiful for God*, two-time Emmy Award winner Anne Petrie's *Mother Teresa—Her Legacy*, Japanese director Shigeki Chiba's *Mother Teresa and Her World*, Anna & Folco Terzani's *Mother Teresa's First Love*, and Dominique LaPierre's *In the Name of God's Poor*. The controversial 1994 *Hell's Angel: Mother Teresa of Calcutta* was also to be shown, but in the end was pulled.

In addition to the film festival, the Vatican issued special commemorative stamps of Mother Teresa. Factories churned out additional merchandise, including Mother Teresa rosaries, crucifixes, and key chains. According to one vendor, his factory is working full time to make 10,000 Mother Teresa rosaries, key chains, and other trinkets. A stage musical and an animated cartoon based on her life and works were to be presented as well. In one of the more bizarre, but also more historically familiar, ways of honoring a holy person, a display of Mother Teresa's blood was planned.

Today, Mother Teresa's thoughts can still be found in the more than 20 books she coauthored to offer spiritual advice and guidance to people. Her order continues to be active and hard at work. Both the sisters and the brothers continue to thrive, though not experiencing the rapid growth of homes and foundations that marked the last 25 years of Mother Teresa's life. More than 3,000 volunteers come to Calcutta every year, hoping to make a difference at least for a little while.

At the same time, the Missionaries of Charity have shown themselves to be a little more worldly, as they successfully copyrighted the name of Mother Teresa in 2003. The nuns said they sought the rights to Mother Teresa's name, the name of their order, and its rosary-encircled globe logo to prevent them from being exploited by commercial interests. It is difficult to say what the future holds for the order; like many other religious orders, the changing climate of the times often forces changes if a religious group hopes to survive. There may be changes in the way the community lives or is administered. There may even be a subtle shift in how best to help the poor, but, as Sister Nirmala comes from a contemplative background—as opposed to a medical or social work emphasis—the direction of the Missionaries of Charity is carried out as Mother Teresa had originally envisioned it.

## THE LEGACY OF MOTHER TERESA

When asked to explain the Missionaries of Charity, Mother Teresa once remarked, "We are first of all religious; we are not social workers, not teachers, not nurses or doctors, we are religious sisters. We serve Jesus in the poor."[14] With that statement, Mother Teresa made clear the mission of the order and to the best of her abilities lived her life following that simple premise.

Still, there is no question that for the last 20 years of her life Mother Teresa and her work were at times seriously misunderstood. She inspired many people not through powerful speeches or magnificent works but because she exemplified a way, imperfect as it was at times, of using the power of love to heal and save. As journalist Mary Poplin pointed out, the key to understanding Mother Teresa and the Missionaries of Charity is the sacredness with which they treat all people and their humble way of carrying out their work. To the Missionaries of Charity, Jesus is present in everyone they meet whether it is a young volunteer from New Jersey or an old Muslim woman starved and half-eaten by rats and worms, or the deformed infant just born and left in a garbage heap. Christ is present in everyone, but most especially in the poorest of the poor. From the very beginning, Mother Teresa and her order reached out to treat each person they encountered as they would Jesus Christ. Thus, they performed each task for the benefit of the poor as they would do it for Christ. In other words, it is Jesus' diapers they wash, his meals they prepare, his ailing body they tend, and his hand being held.

On closer inspection, Mother Teresa appeared a contradiction, a walking paradox, and later, a woman out of step with the times. But that assessment dismisses her and her work much too easily. Mary Poplin, the journalist who volunteered for the Missionaries of Charity, tried to explain her understanding of Mother Teresa:

Many writers have depicted Mother Teresa as someone who
saw the poor and responded sympathetically to their needs.
That is not quite the case. Mother Teresa served the poor not
because they needed her but because God called her to the
work. She was obedient to God's call, not to her social conscience. She often remarked that if God had told her what was
to happen after she picked up the first dying person off the Calcutta street, she would never have done it, for she would have
been too afraid.[15]

Mother Teresa called herself "a pencil in God's hand." What she meant
was that she was simply God's instrument and she did only his bidding, re-
lying on his providence to provide for her order and the poor. Part of her
success lay in her ability to tap into and inspire a large number of volunteers, many of them young men and women who needed help. Quite
often, it was the more knowledgeable and qualified volunteers who had
the most trouble working with and understanding Mother Teresa. But for
many young people who had only high ideals but were not sure how to put
those ideals into practice, Mother Teresa and her work were a good
match. No matter if they stayed an hour, a week, or a year, they were always welcomed. For in the time they stayed, these volunteers made a difference to those around them and Mother Teresa was grateful for their
gifts. For others, Mother Teresa was unique, not because of her work with
the poor, but because for many people, she was doing what they wished to
do. She was what they were not.

Her legacy is strong; at the time of her death, there were more than
4,000 sisters in the Missionaries of Charity, along with 400 brothers and
thousands of others who have volunteered as Co-Workers, Lay Missionaries of Charity, and Missionaries of Charity Fathers. It is through these volunteers that Mother Teresa's spirit lives on. Yet, Mother Teresa had her
flaws as well: she was stubborn, difficult to work with, and demanding.
Perhaps she needed those qualities to carry out the work to which she believed God had called her. But Mother Teresa was also a woman who sang
Happy Birthday to Jesus at Christmas, who regarded all life as holy, and
who saw the face of God in the face of every human being she encountered. For Mother Teresa, her works came not from the strength of her in-
tellect, but of the great power and love she had in her heart.

# NOTES

1. Anne Sebba, *Mother Teresa: Beyond the Image* (New York: Doubleday, 1997), p. 122.

2. "Mother Teresa Dies," BBC Politics 97, http://www.bbc.co.uk/politics97/news/09/0905/teresa.shtml (accessed October 13, 2003).

3. Christoper Hitchens, "Ghoul of Calcutta," *Nation*, April 13, 1992, p. 474.

4. "Mother Teresa: A Profile," CNN Interactive, http://www.cnn.com/WORLD/9709/mother.teresa/profile/ (accessed October 15, 2003).

5. Christopher Hitchens, *The Missionary Position: Mother Teresa In Theory and Practice* (New York: Verso, 1995) p. 7.

6. Christopher Hitchens, *The Missionary Position*, p. 41.

7. Christopher Hitchens, *The Missionary Position*, p. 10.

8. George Sim Johnston, "Mother Teresa and the Missionary Position," review of *The Missionary Position* by Christopher Hitchens in *National Review*, December 25, 1995, p. 58.

9. Bruno Maddox, "The Missionary Position," review of *The Missionary Position* by Christopher Hitchens in *The New York Times Review of Books*, January 14, 1996.

10. Robert Kee, "The Missionary Position," review of *The Missionary Position* by Christopher Hitchens in *The Sunday Times*, November 10, 1995, p. 25.

11. Mary Poplin, "No Humanitarian," *Commonweal*, December 19, 1997, pp. 11–14.

12. Parvathi Menon, "Mother Teresa," *Frontline: India's National Magazine*, September 20–October 3 1997, http://www.frontlineonnet.com/fl1419/14190170.htm.

13. Mary Poplin, "No Humanitarian," pp. 11–14.

14. Nelson Graves, "Mother Teresa No Stranger to Controversy," Reuters: New York, August 24, 1996, http://library.bigchalk.com/cgi-bin/WebObjects/WOPrimo.woa/20/wo/JW75gJ4TBP1s3EEW9q71laknBdo/3.27.2.12.3.

15. Mary Poplin, "No Humanitarian," pp. 11–14.

# BIBLIOGRAPHY

Burgess, Anthony. "Mother Teresa." *Evening Standard,* January 3, 1992.

Chawla, Navin. *Mother Teresa: The Authorized Biography.* Rockport, Mass.: Element, 1992.

Coday, Dennis. "Mother Teresa Trademarked." *National Catholic Reporter,* August 1, 2003, 6.

Cummings, J. "Stubborn Fighter for the Poorest of the Poor." *New York Times Biography Service,* October 1979.

Doig, Desmond. *Mother Teresa, Her People and Her Work.* San Francisco: Harper & Row, 1976.

Egan, Eileen. *The Works of Peace.* New York: Sheed and Ward, 1965.

———. "Mother Teresa: The Myth and the Person." *America,* March 22, 1980, 1238–43.

———. *Such a Vision of the Street: Mother Teresa—The Spirit and the Work.* Garden City, N.Y.: Image Books, 1986.

Gonzales-Balado, Jose. *Always the Poor—Mother Teresa: Her Life and Message.* Liguori, Mo.: Liguori Publications, 1980.

Graves, Nelson. "Mother Teresa No Stranger to Controversy," Reuters: New York, August 24, 1996, http://library.bigchalk.com/cgi-bin/WebObjects/WOPrimo.woa/20/wo/JW75gJ4TBP1s3EEW9q71laknBdo/3.27.2.12.3 (accessed October 14, 2003).

Greer, Germaine. "Heroes and Villains." *Independent,* September 22, 1990.

Hitchens, Christopher. "Ghoul of Calcutta." *Nation,* April 13, 1992, 474.

———. *The Missionary Position: Mother Teresa in Theory and Practice.* New York: Verso Books, 1995.

Johnston, George Sim. "Mother Teresa and the Missionary Position," review of *The Missionary Position by Christopher Hitchens*. *National Review*, December 25, 1995, 58.

Kaufman, M.T. "World of Mother Teresa." *New York Times Magazine*, December 9, 1979, 42–45+.

Kee, Robert. "The Missionary Position," review of *The Missionary Position* by Christopher Hitchens. *Sunday Times*, November 10, 1995, 25.

Le Joly, Edward. *Servant of Love: Mother Teresa and Her Missionaries of Charity*. San Francisco: Harper & Row, 1977.

Maddox, Bruno. "The Missionary Position," review of *The Missionary Position* by Christopher Hutchins. *The New York Times Review of Books*, January 14, 1996, 18.

McGovern, James T. *To Give the Love of Christ: A Portrait of Mother Teresa and the Missionaries of Charity*. New York: Paulist Press, 1978.

Menon, Parvathi. "Mother Teresa." *Frontline: India's National Magazine*, September 20–October 3, 1997," http://www.frontlineonnet.com/fl1419/14190170.htm.

Milestones. *Time International*, August 4, 2003, 17.

"Miracle #1." *U.S. News & World Report*, October 14, 2002, 12.

"Mother Teresa Dies." BBC Politics 97, http://www.bbc.co.uk/politics97/news/09/0905/teresa.shtml (accessed October 10, 2003).

"Mother Teresa: A Profile." CNN Interactive, http://www.cnn.com/WORLD/9709/mother.teresa/profile/ (accessed October 15, 2003).

Muggeridge, Malcolm. *Something Beautiful for God*. San Francisco: Harper & Row, 1971.

Poplin, Mary. "No Humanitarian." *Commonweal*, December 19, 1997, 11–14.

Rae, Daphne. *Love until It Hurts*. San Francisco: Harper & Row, 1981.

Rai, Raghu, and Navin Chawla. *Mother Teresa: Faith and Compassion*. Rockport, Mass.: Element, 1996.

"Saints among Us." *Time*, December 29, 1975, 47–49+.

Sebba, Anne. *Mother Teresa: Beyond the Image*. New York: Doubleday, 1997.

Spink, Kathryn. *Mother Teresa*. San Francisco: Harper & Row, 1997.

Mother Teresa. *A Simple Path*. New York: Ballantine Books, 1995.

————. *Heart of Joy: The Transforming Power of Self-Giving*. Ann Arbor, Mich.: Servant Books, 1987.

————. with Jaya Chaliha and Edward Le Joly. *The Joy in Loving: A Guide to Daily Living*. New York: Viking, 1996.

————. with Jose Luis Gonzàles-Balado. *Mother Teresa: In My Own Words*. New York: Gramercy Books, 1996.

"Thoughts on Mother Teresa." *St. Louis Post-Dispatch*, September 9, 1997, 9A.

"The Week." *National Review*, January 4, 1980, 12.

Woodward, Kenneth. "The Fast Track to Sainthood: How This Diminutive Nun Got Beatified a Record Seven Years after Her Death." *Newsweek,* October 20, 2003, 52.

## WEB SITES

Mother Teresa: Angel of Mercy, http://www.cnn.com/WORLD/9709/mother. teresa/

Nobel Museum: Mother Teresa, http://www.nobel.se/peace/laureates/1979/ teresa-bio.html

Nobel Prize Internet Archive: Mother Teresa, http://almaz.com/nobel/peace/ 1979a.html

Paying Tribute to Mother Teresa, http://www.americancatholic.org/Features/ teresa/

*Time* Magazine 100 Heroes and Icons: Mother Teresa, http://www.time.com/time/ time100/heroes/profile/teresa01.html

# INDEX

## About the Author

MEG GREENE is an independent scholar and author of many books for young adults.